THE STORY OF AUSTRALIA

This special edition is printed and distributed by arrangement with the originators and publishers of Landmark Books, RANDOM HOUSE, Inc., New York, by

E. M. HALE AND COMPANY
EAU CLAIRE, WISCONSIN

THE STORY OF
AUSTRALIA

by A. Grove Day

illustrated by W. R. Lohse

CONTENTS

THE STORY OF AUSTRALIA

WESTE

AUSTRA

Perth

Torres Strait

Possession I.

Darwin

CAPE YORK PENINSULA

Endeavor R.

Great Barrier Reef

NORTHERN
TERRITORY

QUEENSLAND

stralia

A

SOUTH

AUSTRALIA

NEW SOUTH

WALES

Darling R.

Lachlan R.

Murray R.

Murrumbidgee R.

Blue Mts.

Sydney

Adelaide

Botany
Bay

Brisbane

VICTORIA

Ballarat Bendigo

Melbourne

Port
Phillip

Bass Strait

Macquarie
Harbor

TASMANIA

Derwent R.

Hobart

1   *The Dark Discoverers*

A thousand miles of ocean lie between Australia and the Asian mainland. It was not always so. Scientists tell us that Australia was once part of Asia. Hundreds of millions of years ago, they say, the island continent broke off and slid away. And there, far in the south, it lay while mighty forces shaped it.

Mountains rose along the eastern coast. Time and again glaciers covered them. Volcanoes thundered and burst. Sea rolled where there is no sea today. Life came. In the great ice ages, when the level of the ocean sank, strange pouched animals walked into Australia over the land bridges. Quite recently

—mere thousands of years ago—the sea made a channel across the southeastern tip, which became the island we call Tasmania.

Then men discovered Australia. Today some scientists believe that the earliest Australians arrived in two waves. Perhaps, like the animals, the first men came over the land bridges from the islands. They may have been dark-skinned, fuzzy-haired people, who used rough chips of stone for tools. Their spears were pointed sticks hardened in the fire, with no head of stone or bone. The people wore no clothes. Sometimes for shelter they crept into hollow trees. Sometimes they stuck a few branches in the ground to break the wind.

Nobody knows when these first dark discoverers came into Australia. Certainly it was long ago. For thousands of years they lived in the land—hunting, gathering food, eating shellfish, and piling up the shells in great heaps. The simple, peaceful people melted into the land. They became as much a part of it as the animals they hunted. The bridges over which they crossed had disappeared, and the all-surrounding ocean kept them a secret from the world.

Then—some scientists think—on the islands to the north and west of the continent a pushing began. Strong men were driving out weaker ones.

The weak were a chocolate-colored people with wavy, not fuzzy, hair. They were related to the dark hill-people of southern India. Their skulls were very thick. They had heavy eyebrow ridges on foreheads that sloped sharply back. Their chins sloped back, too, and their noses spread very wide at the tip. They were a Stone Age people, not very far advanced, but they had canoes. So when it came to life or death, they got into their craft and set out for the unknown. And with them went the dingo, the wolflike dog that afterward went wild.

Somehow they stumbled on Australia. It was so barren a land that nobody else seemed to want it —except the fuzzy-haired men who had come before them. But that timid folk put up no sort of resistance. They fled from the invaders, who were much more advanced than they—fled farther and farther south till the last of them crossed over into Tasmania, which remained wholly theirs.

The new discoverers pushed out over the continent. They spread in groups all around the coasts and went down the rivers and across some of the deserts. The separate groups became tribes and sub-tribes. As always happens when people live apart, language differences sprang up, and at last the five hundred or more tribes each spoke a different language or dialect.

They didn't ask much of the land, these second dark discoverers of Australia. They needed little. They wore no clothes; they wanted no shelter. Their stone-headed spears brought down game. Some tribes had the boomerang—a cleverly curved stick that would come back if it failed to strike its object. Their nets caught fish. With their digging sticks they could get up yams and roots. And there were grass seeds to gather and grind into flour. It never occurred to these primitive people that plants grow from seeds. So they knew nothing of planting. They picked the wild mangoes. They collected turtle eggs. They gathered shellfish and wild honey

8

and witchetty grubs—a kind of insect larva. They lived on what nature gave them ready-made.

In most ways nature was not bountiful. For there was very little rainfall on this continent. But the Australoids—as scientists would one day call these people—had no domestic animals that needed grass. Food was often scarce; yet whatever they had each tribe shared with all their people. The old, the sick, the young each had a share even when there was only a mouthful apiece. In the regions where kangaroos abounded nobody needed to go hungry. And there were many animals besides the kangaroo—koala bear and wombat and bandicoot and smaller creatures.

The people took what nature gave them and believed that supernatural beings had provided it all. They gave much thought to those supernatural beings. They thought yet more about their ancestors, weaving endless myths and legends about them. Each tribe had its own myths and its own mysteries. It took a boy many years to get initiated into all the mysteries of his tribe.

The people almost never fought over land or

possessions. What could be taken from their neighbors? A bark tray, a wooden drinking vessel, a rude bucket—that was about all anyone had besides his tools of polished stone and his weapons. The land was very large, and in all of it there were perhaps only 300,000 people. There was room enough for all. Every tribe knew its own boundaries and didn't want to live anywhere but in its own homeland. For that was the land of its ancestors, the land where its mythical heroes had had their adventures. Everyone wanted his children to be born where those wonderful adventures had taken place. The most important things in life were myth and legend and the singing and dancing that went with them. The sacred get-togethers—the corroborees—were very frequent under the stars. There song and story, dancing and acting took up the minds and hearts of the people and lifted them out of themselves.

So they lived for perhaps thousands of years, on their island continent. The all-encircling ocean protected them and shut them from the world, as it protected and shut in from the world the yet more primitive Tasmanians in their island to the south.

Australia, the Island Continent.
Every tribe had its own myths and legends.

2 *The Unknown South Land*

Australia lay remote and unsuspected. And yet, as the centuries passed, scholars in Europe came to believe that the southern ocean was not all empty.

"There must be a continent in the southern hemisphere," they said. "There has to be—to balance the weight of Europe and Asia in the north. Otherwise the earth would be lopsided."

The scholars even gave a Latin name to the continent—*Terra Australis Incognita,* the Unknown South Land.

In the early 1600's the Dutch, who had come as traders to the Spice Islands, finally discovered Australia. To them it was an extremely disappointing land. They found no gold, no spices, not so much as a single fruit tree. What was the good of a land like that?

An Englishman named Dampier heartily agreed with the Dutch in their opinion of New Holland, as the continent came to be called. He reported it to be the most barren spot on the globe. Its inhabitants, he said, were "the miserablest people in the world." "The Hottentots," he said, "though a nasty people, are gentlemen compared with these, who, setting aside their human shape, differ but little from the brutes."

But was New Holland the same as the Unknown South Land?

King George III of England, along with a lot of other people, did not believe it. No, somewhere in the South Seas lay another continent, a much better continent doubtless. King George wanted it found. Englishmen should take possession of the land in his name before somebody else laid claim to it.

For several years, nothing was done about the mysterious continent. But in 1768, George III at

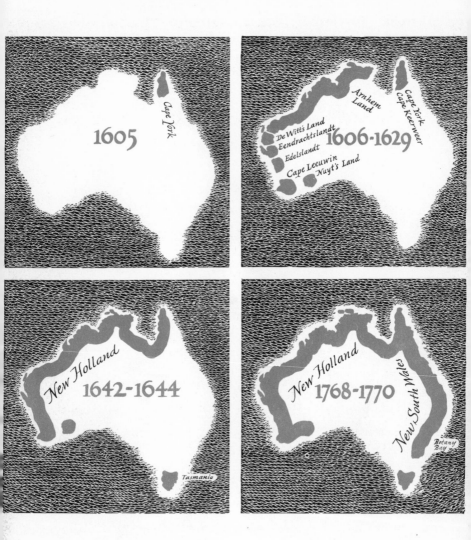

The exploration of the Australian coastline took almost two centuries, from the first Dutch discovery (1605) to Matthew Flinders' voyage around the continent (1803).

1788-1803
Australia

Port
Jackson
(Sydney)

last saw his chance to add Terra Australis Incognita to his possessions.

Before him lay a petition from a scientific society. An astronomical event of the greatest importance was about to happen: the planet Venus was going to cross the face of the sun. Such a transit of Venus would not be seen again for over a hundred years, and the event should be observed from somewhere in the Pacific. Would His Majesty grant funds for a ship to transport scholars and their instruments to the island of Tahiti?

King George agreed. But he also gave secret instructions that the ship's captain should find the Unknown South Land and take possession of it.

So the *Endeavor* was provisioned for a long voyage, James Cook was put in command, and the ship with its scientists sailed off to Tahiti. The chief of the three scientists was Joseph Banks, a noted botanist. Besides his four servants, he was bringing with him four artists, a small library, and all sorts of scientific equipment. He was spending twice as much money on the expedition as was the king.

Captain Cook carried out his instructions. When

the transit of Venus had been observed, he sailed fifteen hundred miles south and looked for the mysterious continent. He couldn't find it.

"Perhaps New Zealand is part of a continent," the captain thought. So he sailed all around it. But no, New Zealand was two big islands and a little one.

By this time Captain Cook was positive that Terra Australis Incognita existed only in people's imagination. He prepared to go home. "But first," he thought, "I will head directly west. If I do that, I am bound to come to the east coast of New Holland. It has never been explored or mapped. And in my opinion, except for the frozen land around the Pole, New Holland is the only South Land there is."

On April 20, 1770, the continent was sighted. On the 29th, Captain Cook anchored the *Endeavor* off the coast. Because of the presence of great numbers of stingrays there, he called the place Stingray Harbor. But later, when he realized the importance of all the new plants that Joseph Banks and his company collected on the spot, he changed the name to Botany Bay. On August 22, on a little island to which he gave the name of Possession, Captain Cook ran up the British flag and in the name of his king took possession of the whole east coast of New Holland. He called it New South Wales.

3 *The Sailing of the First Fleet*

A vast new territory had suddenly been acquired by England. But what could be done with this land "down under," on the other side of the earth, half a world away?

For a while nothing was done. Then came the American Revolution, and thousands of British men and women went sailing to New South Wales.

What was the connection?

It lay in the fact that for a long time England had been using the American colonies as a dumping ground for her convicts. She had been sending over about a thousand a year. Now that the American colonies had declared themselves independent, no more convicts could be dumped there, and some other place had to be found—quickly. For the jails of England were overflowing.

But why were there so many criminals?

Some were professional thieves and highwaymen. But also times were hard. The towns were full of starving people, and starving people will steal to eat and feed their loved ones. Moreover, the temptation to break the law was great because there was a good chance of escaping punishment. For only in London was there anything like a real police.

"Do something about it!" respectable citizens urged. "Nobody can feel safe in the street after dark. Nobody can feel safe even in his bed!"

The government could think of just one thing to do—punish the lawbreakers so severely that others would be afraid to commit crimes. So the laws became very cruel. More than two hundred crimes were punishable by death. And many of them were trifling. The penalty for stealing more than a shilling—about twenty-five cents—out of somebody's pocket was death. Death was the penalty for poaching, for damaging trees, for stealing oysters, for killing butcher's meat without a license.

For many crimes the punishment was transportation—being sent away to a far-off land and forced to work for years without pay, under the lash, for some master whose only interest in his "slave" was to get as much work out of him as possible. If a man with friends and influence committed a crime for which the punishment was death, it was often changed to transportation. But transportation was also imposed for the smallest of crimes. A woman could be sent across the sea for stealing a handkerchief. Even a ten-year-old child could be transported for a trifle. Many twelve- and thirteen-year-old boys and girls were transported, and one boy only seven years old was transported for life. Transportation was an easy way to get rid of people who were problems. A man might be transported for recommending that everybody have the right to vote, or for advising workers to stand up for their rights.

The convict problem was giving the authorities trouble. There was no place to put them any more! Some old, rotting ships were fitted out on the River

Thames, but these old hulks, too, were quickly filled with convicts waiting to be transported. And the conditions in these old ships were horrible. Loaded with chains, in rags and covered with vermin, the despairing prisoners raved and filled the air with their screams and groans.

What was to be done? Jail fever carried off hundreds, but still there were thousands upon thousands of convicts left. And the government had to pay the jailer sixpence a day to feed each one.

Boatloads of miserable creatures were transported to the fever-ridden coast of Africa. But the guards died as well as the convicts, and that made trouble at home.

Joseph Banks, who had sailed with Captain Cook in the *Endeavor,* made a proposal. He remembered fondly his stay in Botany Bay, where he had found so many strange plants. Convicts sent there, he told the authorities, might earn their keep by raising hemp for rope-making. The soil was good and timber abundant. And one thing was sure—nobody could escape from New South Wales.

Those in authority thought it over. The plan certainly had a major advantage: it was so far away that no convict would stand a chance of getting back to England. Send the lot to Botany Bay! England would be rid of her rascals forever! Besides, what cheaper way of getting rid of the convicts could be found? It cost nearly £27 (twenty-seven pounds) a year to keep one in the hulks. It would cost only £17 to get him over to New South Wales.

But who should go out with the prisoners and govern the colony?

The choice fell on Captain Arthur Phillip, a retired naval officer, who had taken up farming in the south of England.

The captain was as surprised as anybody else when he was asked to head the "First Fleet" to settle New South Wales. But it was not the sort of thing a man of his character could refuse. He had served his country before, and here was a great opportunity to do it again. He believed in reforming men, not simply punishing them. He had a vision of a colony where men and women who had broken the law would learn to uphold it. He saw green fields, fruit trees, stock, neat houses.

Phillip threw himself into the task of supplying the ships; for the colonists would have to live at least two years on what they brought out. He refused to leave until he received a stock of the most badly needed things. But the quality of the food, clothing, and tools he got was worse than that of goods used for trade with the African natives. Anything was good enough for convicts going to Botany Bay!

At last all was ready. Clanking their heavy locks and fetters, the long lines of convicts filed down to Portsmouth dock. Governor Phillip's heart sank when he saw them. He had asked for carefully selected convicts fitted for farm work. He had been given the least desirable convicts, the sick, the old, the crippled, the unmanageable—those whom the jailers most wanted to get rid of. One woman was over eighty years old.

On the 13th of May, 1787, the First Fleet set sail. It consisted of a frigate, an armed tender, three store ships, and six transports filled with convicts. Eight months later the ships reached New South Wales.

But was this indeed Botany Bay, which Joseph Banks had recommended with such assurance? As the governor explored the desolate-looking shore, with its dreary sand dunes and swamps, he found it hard to believe he had come to the right place. This seemed to him the worst possible site for a town. Nothing would grow in those swamps and dunes. Moreover there was no wood and no fresh water handy. And the anchorage was shallow.

He embarked to go sailing up the coast. And eight days later the entrance to a great harbor opened before him. Captain Cook had not explored it but had given it the name of Port Jackson.

For the first time since setting out, Governor Phillip saw something to be enthusiastic about. "This is the finest harbor in the world," he thought. "A thousand ships of the line may ride here in the most perfect security." He landed in a snug cove. A small stream of fresh water flowed near by. There were many trees.

The occasion called for something special. The governor hoisted the British flag and ordered three cheers to be given for the king. Evening was ap-

proaching. On this spot—where the great city of Sydney now stands with more than two million inhabitants—the convicts began gathering sticks, building fires, and cooking their evening meal.

The first settlers raised the British flag.

4 *Governor Phillip and the New Colony*

Next morning the animals that had survived the long journey were brought ashore. The tools were found. Everything needed to be done at once, but shelter was first in the governor's mind. Convicts were set to work chopping down the strange trees of the strange land.

But now came the first disappointment. A dozen men knew something about carpentry. Yet when they tried to use the wood, they found it was not fit for building. For months to come the governor would have to live in a canvas hut, while the convicts would be without shelter. There were no blankets. When storms came, they would shiver in their rags.

With sinking heart, Governor Phillip from day to day saw his wretched equipment fall apart and observed how unskilled and shiftless the convicts were. The fishing nets had rotted. The axes, the spades, and the shovels would take no strain. There was not a single plow for this colony that was expected to raise its own food. And only one man knew anything about farming—Phillip's own manservant.

As for the land, it looked pleasant enough. But no country, the governor thought, could offer less help to first settlers than this one. Where were the meadows that Captain Cook had reported? The soil was not fertile. It was just black sand. As soon as the trees were cut down and the ground was exposed to the sun, the earth dried and the grass cover shriveled. Nothing would grow in soil like that. The pretty, parklike appearance of the country was a deceit: the land was barren. There were no vegetables, no native grain, nothing deserving the name of fruit. The wood was fit only for the fire. There was no kind of plant from which rope could be made, as Joseph Banks had so confidently suggested. Nor, as far as anyone could see, was there any metal.

The marines and officers who had come to guard the convicts looked about them with even more gloom. Everything was so different from England. Where were the sparkling streams of their home-land? Where were the dependable rains that made everything fresh and green? The land was dry, dry. The plants were all so odd, too. The trees did not spread their leaves horizontally as at home, but hung straight down, turning only their edges to the sun. The scanty foliage remained throughout the year, pale and without sheen. Instead of a shed-ding of leaves, there seemed to be a shedding of bark. It hung in long, untidy strings, giving the woods a desolate look.

The animals, too, except for one that looked like a wolf, were all peculiar. They carried their young about in pouches. There were no deer, no rabbits, nothing the Englishmen were accustomed to hunt. The insects were terrible pests. Mosquitoes and flies were everywhere. A man had to keep moving his arms to keep the bugs from getting into his eyes and nose. The bite of the ants stung and burned. And there was a provoking bird that sounded just as if it were laughing at the misfortunes of the newcomers.

The country frightened the settlers. Nothing was the way it ought to be. Even the seasons were upside down, so that Christmas came in the middle of summer.

Governor Phillip had to call on all his inner strength. He tried to take a long view. "Things will get better," he told himself. "Time will remove all difficulties."

But time passed and things grew worse. The convicts scratched the earth between the stumps with their hoes, but nothing grew the way it should. There was no manure to improve the wretched soil. For the cattle had strayed away, and the grass was so poor that after six months only one sheep was left alive. Fifty-two of the convicts were too old or too infirm to work. Most of the rest tried to shirk. The women convicts mostly lived in a state of utter idleness.

As for the marines, they would do nothing but guard duty. They wouldn't even act as overseers, so that the governor had to set convicts to oversee the work of other convicts. Major Ross, chief of the marines, who should have been Phillip's right-hand man, spent all his time either complaining or flogging the convicts. Flogging seemed to be the only thing that gave him satisfaction. In the end, after two years of bearing with him and his cruelties, the governor sent the major off to rule Norfolk Island, a settlement that had been started a month after the landing. It lay about a thousand miles northeast of Sydney. Flax grew wild there, Phillip had been told. But this, too, proved a myth.

Sickness plagued Phillip's colony. In the first six months, twenty-eight convicts and eight children died. The governor was grim, haunted by fear of starvation. "We must have a regular supply of provisions for four or five years," he wrote home. "The crops for two years to come cannot be depended on for more than will be necessary for seed."

Surely England would not let her erring sons and daughters die of hunger in this inhospitable land.

Slow starvation settled on Sydney. Each convict's weekly ration of flour, dry peas, worm-eaten rice, and rancid salt pork grew so small that it went in two meals. People stole from the storehouses to keep alive. Everybody stole, even the marines. The governor hanged those he caught. But that did not stop the stealing. When the wheat crop of 1789 failed and still no ship came, despair took hold of the pioneers. The great world had forgotten them. Then on June 2, 1790, two and a half years after the landing, the hungry watchers saw a vessel approaching. Food! All who were able ran to the shore. Men and women wept for joy.

But the new ship, the *Lady Juliana,* bore no food. She brought 221 women convicts. To the cries of "What news? What news?" came a terrible answer: "The supply ship was wrecked off the Cape of Good Hope. A thousand convicts more are on the way."

They arrived—not all of the thousand, for 267 had died on the voyage out. The others were in a desperate condition. Almost a hundred died in the six weeks that followed, while the rest were too weak to work.

33

More mouths to feed—with what? More useless convicts. How could a self-supporting settlement ever be built by such as these? Governor Phillip wrote letter after letter to England. "Send healthy free settlers who know how to run a farm or a factory," he pleaded. All he got was another two thousand sick and miserable convicts.

But the governor had not just waited for help from England. Fifteen miles up the harbor from Sydney, fertile land had been discovered. Governor Phillip had started farming it for the colony. Moreover, he had made a policy of granting land to convicts whose terms had expired. Quite a number were now working land for themselves. And it was wonderful to see what freedom and their own land were doing for them. Shiftlessness had vanished. They were different human beings.

Uneasily the dark inhabitants of the land watched the white men and their doings. The natives could not understand all this scratching of soil. Indeed, there was not much they could understand. The white men covered up their bodies and puffed smoke from their mouths and carried thunder sticks. Their magic was very strong. Strange animals obeyed them and birds pecked the ground at their feet.

The settlers for their part despised the natives. Ugly, naked creatures who didn't know enough even to desire possessions! But Governor Phillip did not share this general feeling. He had named a nearby place Manly because he admired the manly way in which the natives behaved. He had a deep respect for them. "They are able to feed themselves in a land where we white men are starving," he thought. "They can find water where we would die of thirst. They are better hunters with poorer weapons—and they are happier men."

Captain Cook had been impressed with the fact that the native people of New Holland were not warlike. He had thought them "a timorous and inoffensive race, no ways inclined to cruelty." And Governor Phillip had striking proof that this was so.

He had given commands that all his people should treat the natives well. Nevertheless a convict in Sydney was caught stealing some fishing tackle from a native woman—one Daringa. The governor decided to make an example of him.

"The rascal shall be severely flogged in the presence of as many natives as can be got together," he said. "They shall see for themselves that I will not tolerate their being mistreated in any way."

Accordingly many natives were assembled, both men and women, and the reason for the punishment was explained to them. But as soon as the flogging began, there was an outcry from the natives. They could not bear to look on at the white man's cruelty. Not one but showed his sympathy with the sufferer. Daringa herself broke into tears. Another woman snatched a stick and tried to drive away the men with the whips.

The governor did his best to establish good relations. But nothing he said or did could get his men to act with humanity toward these strangely soft-hearted natives. Behind his back they were cruelly mistreated, and it was not long before the natives understood that the white man was an enemy. Phillip himself became a victim of their fear. One day when the governor was on a visit to a nearby tribe, a native hurled his spear into the governor's shoulder. True to his principles, Arthur Phillip would not let his marines punish the man. But from that time on he had a foreboding about the future. There would be neither peace nor understanding between these men to whom the land belonged and his own people who had come to take it way from them.

At the time the governor was recovering from his wound, the colony's affairs were in very bad shape, for the crops had suffered from drought. But in the spring of 1791 he received wonderful news. James Ruse, a former convict and the first man to whom he had granted land, declared that he could now raise enough food on his thirty acres to support himself.

A great load fell from the governor's shoulders when he heard that. He knew that hungry times were still ahead. Yet this was his happiest moment since he had sailed into the beautiful harbor. "It is the beginning," he told himself.

It was. When in the following year Governor Phillip gave up his commission and sailed for Eng-

The first successful farmer was an ex-convict.

land, his colony was farming more than two thousand acres of land and feeding itself. Besides this, more than four thousand acres that had been granted to settlers were being worked by convict labor. In a land that offered little more than space, out of perhaps the poorest human material on earth, Arthur Phillip had built a colony that could stand on its own feet. He did not guess that one day he would be called the "father of the Australian nation." But he had a glowing vision of the future of New South Wales.

"It will yet prove the most valuable acquisition Great Britain ever made," he thought, as Port Jackson faded from his sight.

5   *Rum Corps Rebellion*

The good start made by Governor Phillip didn't last long. He had scarcely turned his back when the "Rum Corps" began to make serious trouble for the colony.

The real name of this infamous outfit was the New South Wales Corps. It had been sent out to guard the settlement. But its officers, who were the riffraff of the British army, quickly turned their job into racketeering. They worked out a wonderful get-rich-quick scheme that gave them power in New South Wales.

In the early days, when the colony was short of

everything, any trading vessel that came to Sydney could sell its cargo to the colonists for fantastic prices. The officers thought this outrageous.

"Why should we let the masters of ships get away with it?" the officers said among themselves. "Why shouldn't *we* be the ones to make the profit? When a ship comes in, let us buy up its entire cargo ourselves. Then we will sell it to the colonists for what we please."

This is exactly what they did. As soon as a ship came in, they would go on board, buy up everything, then sell it for five times as much. Sometimes they sold goods for ten times their cost.

The colonists were helpless. The only regular market the farmers could sell to was the government store. But the governors were not wise enough to buy reserves for the future. When they had bought enough to feed the convicts for the time being, they closed the store. So the farmers were forced to sell to the officers, who were always ready to buy. When crops failed, as in this land of drought and floods they were bound to, the officers would get an enormous price for the stored wheat. Meantime they didn't pay the farmers in money. The officers forced them to take in exchange whatever was on hand, things the farmers didn't really want, things they considered luxuries—tea, sugar, wine, liquor, fancy waistcoats, and silk handkerchiefs.

The same was true of laborers. The same was true of soldiers. They had to take what the officers gave them.

A soldier would come in to the captain to get his month's pay.

"Well, what do you want?" the captain would say.

"I want to be paid, sir."

"What will you have? I have very good tobacco, and good tea, and print cloth."

"Sir, I do not want any of your goods," the soldier would say.

"You don't?" the captain would reply. "You are a saucy rascal! Begone, you mutinous scoundrel, or I'll send you to the guardhouse and have you flogged for your impertinence to an officer."

The soldier would have to take his pay in things he didn't want. Then he would try to sell them to someone else for half the price.

The worst of it was that the New South Wales Corps began to deal more and more in liquor. And that's how it got the name of Rum Corps. Masters of American ships learned they could sell rum in Sydney. They came loaded with it. The Rum Corps bought it all. Some of the officers also distilled their own and sold it. A convict working in his free time was paid for his labor in rum. A soldier got his pay in rum. A farmer sold his year's crop for rum; in one riotous week he would drink up all his year's earnings. When he got into debt, he was encouraged to sell his land for rum.

The result was drunkenness, riot, and ruin everywhere. The small landowners lost their property to the members of the Rum Corps, who acquired more and more land, until the community was virtually in the hands of a score or so of farming officers.

One of the richest of these rum-dealing farmers was John Macarthur, an unscrupulous and quarrelsome fellow who was farming his land with great skill. He had fruit trees and stock and much grain. He was also doing something that nobody else was —breeding sheep that would bear good wool. Others besides Macarthur bred sheep. But these men were interested in more meat, not better fleece.

In 1794 Macarthur had no sheep. Four years later he had six hundred. A few of them were Spanish sheep, merinos, that bore very fine wool and had been brought from South Africa. Macarthur was very careful to keep the breed pure. Soon he had a third of all the sheep in New South Wales, and they were the very best in the quality of their fleece.

Governor Hunter had struggled with Macarthur. It had ended in the governor's recall. Now Governor King was trying to break the power of the Rum Corps. He put a duty on every gallon of liquor and wine.

Macarthur struck back by breaking off social relations with the governor and persuading other officers to do the same. "Have nothing to do with him," Macarthur urged. "That will bring him around." When Paterson, the commander of the Rum Corps, refused, Macarthur fought a duel and wounded him.

Here was the governor's chance. He arrested Macarthur and let him be sent to England for a court-martial. "If ever Captain Macarthur returns to this colony," the governor wrote, "I shall feel much for its concerns. Half of it belongs to him already, and he will very soon get the other half."

But Macarthur arrived in England at exactly the right moment.

England was fighting a war with Napoleon. The supply of fine wool from Spain and Saxony, on which the English weavers depended for their best, had been cut off. Many weavers were idle. Macarthur brought out samples of his wool.

"In a few years I shall be turning out tons of wool as good as that of Spain and Saxony," he boasted.

Those in authority paid attention. There was no question that Macarthur's samples of merino wool were just as good as the best Spanish. What folly to court-martial a man who could raise such wool! Here was a chance to make New South Wales pay back all it had cost the crown. The ships that took convicts and supplies to the colony could come back laden with fine wool, wool that would save the British industry.

45

In June 1805, Governor King saw his enemy come sailing back into Sydney Harbor in his own ship, which he had named the *Argo*. On board were five purebred merino sheep from the royal flock of King George III. In Macarthur's pocket was an order for a grant of five thousand acres of the best land in New South Wales and the use of thirty convicts to work for him as shepherds.

Macarthur's wife Elizabeth, a woman of sense and education, had kept the farm going while he was away. Now they went to work together on their

John and Elizabeth Macarthur bred sheep for fine wool.

new estate. With his additional acres, Macarthur was the richest man in Australia.

Governor King had lost out. He was recalled, and Captain William Bligh was sent to replace him.

The new governor had been chosen for one single reason: he was considered the ideal man to break the rum traffic. As a sea captain, William Bligh had shown great firmness, courage, and endurance. When the crew of the *Bounty* had mutinied and set him and his faithful men in an open boat in the middle of the Pacific, Captain Bligh had made a journey of 3168 miles, landing safely on the island of Timor.

Bligh was tough and unyielding. He had come determined to help the colonists. He struck again and again at those who had grown fat on the drunkenness of the people.

Macarthur was tough and unyielding too. A showdown was bound to come, and very soon it did—on several counts. One was that a convict escaped on a schooner belonging to Macarthur. Another was that a still had been brought to Sydney for him. The governor was not going to let anyone make liquor. He ordered the still seized. When Macarthur defied him, Bligh had him arrested.

Six officers of the Rum Corps and the government judge, Atkins, were appointed to try Macarthur. But the prisoner didn't like the judge and objected to his sitting on the case. Atkins withdrew. Bligh, however, wouldn't let the trial go on without the judge.

"There is going to be trouble," the governor said to Lieutenant Colonel Johnston, the head of the Corps. "I want you to help me keep order."

Johnston's answer was to go to the barracks and let Macarthur out of jail.

After that things happened fast. Macarthur persuaded Johnston to arrest Bligh and take over the government. With loaded muskets and fixed bayonets, and with the band playing "The British Grenadiers," the New South Wales Corps marched four hundred strong to Bligh's house. They captured him as he was hiding papers under his bed.

The rebels were triumphant. They kept Bligh under arrest for a year before they let him sail away. For another year, they ruled the colony.

Macarthur, who held a post without pay, was really in charge. But this couldn't go on. England could not let the officers get away with their Rum Rebellion. The New South Wales Corps was replaced. A new governor was sent out. And John Macarthur had to go to England to explain his part in the mutiny.

He was not allowed to return for nine years. In his absence Elizabeth Macarthur managed the two farms. When her husband at last came home, she was able to show him a flock of 5500 sheep.

But something more important had happened meanwhile. Macarthur's idea of an Australian wool industry had taken hold. Wool was the ideal export for this land where convicts could be made to work as shepherds for nothing. Wool didn't spoil on the way to market. Wool could be carried without harm over lonely tracks on big, jolting carts drawn by bullocks. It could be taken thousands of miles by water in damp ships and yet arrive in London in good condition. Plenty of good pasture was the chief thing a great wool industry called for. And after 1813 there was no question that Australia had that.

6 *Beyond the Blue Mountains*

For twenty-five years, the convict colony remained shut in between the sea and the mountains. Those high Blue Mountains seemed to be an impassable barrier. Dark, sheer, and rugged, they rose behind the settlement, like the wall of a jail. No one could find a way through. The valleys seemed to lead nowhere. Always the baffled explorers would come to a dead end, ringed in by high, steep sandstone cliffs.

In the beginning men had tried to cross the Blue Mountains just for curiosity. There was fertile land enough this side of the ranges. But as the colony grew and sheep multiplied, people began to look ahead. And when the drought of 1813 came, crossing the mountains became a matter of life and death. For the grass was nearly all destroyed, the water had failed, and the horned cattle were dying in great numbers.

Gregory Blaxland, a large landowner, determined to try to get across. He asked Lieutenant Lawson and William Wentworth, the twenty-year-old son of the biggest landowner in New South Wales, to go along. Blaxland had a plan that he believed would give them a fair chance to pass the mountains.

"I am not going to follow the valleys as others have done," he said. "I mean to go along the ridges. I have found a man who hunts kangaroos in the mountains, and he has agreed to take the horses to the top of the first ridge."

So with four servants, five dogs, and four horses laden with provisions and ammunition, the explorers crossed the western river and climbed to the top of the first knifelike ridge. It was very crooked and narrow. On either side of them, deep rocky gullies dropped down. The ground was covered with trees and scrubby brushwood, very thick in places. The going was so hard that the explorers had to go first to clear the scrub. Then they went back to take the horses through. Slow, discouraging work it was, some three miles a day, but they persisted. And at last on the ninth day they reached the top of the third ridge. Now they could look back and see the settlement eighteen miles away. What was more exciting, they could look down toward the west and see the land beyond the mountains.

At first they were disappointed. From the great height of the ridge the country below seemed to be sandy and barren. But when they had got their horses down the steep descent, to their great joy they found themselves in clear meadowland with grass two to three feet high and a stream flowing through. They went on. A high sugar-loaf hill was before them. They scrambled up and stood drinking in the scene, thrilled by the sense of discovery. All around them were forest and grass.

"There is enough grassland here to support the stock of the colony for the next thirty years," Blaxland said triumphantly.

The explorers would have pushed farther, but

53

their provisions were nearly gone, their clothes and shoes were in very bad shape, and the whole party was sick. They decided to turn back.

"We've done the important thing anyway," young Wentworth said. "There is nothing now to keep the colony from expanding westward. A road will be built right along the track we have cleared. It's all marked out."

The three men rejoiced because they had opened the gate to the interior, but they realized they had only made a dent in the job of exploration. They had not gone even a hundred miles into the un-

Bold explorers showed the way through the Blue Mountains.

known, and a whole continent lay beyond the mountains. What was that continent like? Was it flat or was it mountainous? Perhaps Australia was two islands with a strait between. Perhaps the center of the continent was a sea.

A surveyor named Evans lifted a corner of the mystery soon afterwards. He found two rivers flowing away from the coast. He called them the Macquarie and the Lachlan. But where did they go? Did they empty into the ocean to the north or the ocean to the south? Or did they run into a central sea?

John Oxley, another surveyor, tried in vain to find the answer. He traced the rivers many miles, but they disappeared in an impassable swamp. He found and traced a third river. It disappeared in an "ocean of reeds" that he could neither go through nor go around.

"Most likely those reeds are the outskirts of a great inland sea into which the rivers empty," Oxley thought.

But who would find out?

Let the matter lie! There were many more pressing problems than exploring a useless bog!

7 *Captain Sturt Explores the Rivers*

Captain Charles Sturt was a young army officer who had been sent to escort convicts to New South Wales. He had gone out thinking he would hate Australia. To his surprise, the climate, the scenery, and the new spirit of this land where anything might happen to a man all captivated him. A new, tall, clear-eyed generation was growing up. The parents of these native-born Australians were mostly homesick convicts to whom Australia still seemed strange. But the sons and daughters of the land had no fear of it. The boys grew up skilled bushmen. Not for them the dull work of shepherds! They became horse breakers, cattle drovers, bullock teamsters, sheep shearers. Sturt admired these self-reliant lads who could find their way without a compass, survive where others would die, and live all their years on the road and in the remote camps.

But most especially was the young officer's mind stirred by the mystery of the inland. He wanted desperately to find out the geography of the new continent. Its coast had already been mapped. Twenty-five years earlier, Matthew Flinders, then a young man with as much curiosity as Sturt himself, had sailed all around the continent and made splendid charts. But of the interior very little was known.

So in 1828, when a three-year drought had caused much suffering, Sturt offered to go on an expedition of discovery. Governor Darling gladly accepted, for along the coast there was neither pasture nor water left.

Hamilton Hume, who had discovered many miles of fine country in the south, agreed to go along as Sturt's right-hand man. Hume had been born in Australia. He knew a good deal about the ways of the natives, and he proceeded to teach Sturt how to get on with them.

"You must never be in a hurry with the natives," Hume said. "You must give them time to get used to seeing white men and strange beasts. You have to make allowance for customs and prejudices."

"I will," thought Charles Sturt. And aloud he said, "I don't want any bloodshed. Let us be just to the natives and show that we admire justice in them."

He led the expedition right along John Oxley's tracks. But it was as though they were in a different country. Oxley had traced the rivers in a wet season; Sturt was doing it in a dry one, and this made all the difference. The "ocean of reeds" the surveyor had seen had shrunk greatly. In place of the sea which those reeds were supposed to fringe, there was only a waterless waste. Everything was parched. The ostrich-like emus with outstretched necks gasped with thirst as they vainly searched for water in the river channels. The native dogs, so thin that they could hardly walk, seemed to beg the explorers to put them out of their misery.

Sturt pressed on while the unbearable heat increased and increased. The thermometer seldom read under 114 degrees at noon and rose still higher by 2 P.M. The ground was so dry that large cracks had opened up in it.

Was there only parched earth ahead? One day, seeing a native path trodden like a road, Sturt followed it toward some giant trees that showed in the distance. Suddenly the astonished party drew up on a bank above a noble river. It was seventy to eighty yards broad and was covered with pelicans and other wild fowl. The bank was too far above the stream for the horses to get to the water, but all the men except Sturt eagerly scrambled down.

Afterward Sturt could never forget the cry of amazement that came up to him or the looks of terror and disappointment with which the men called out, "Captain Sturt, it is as salty as the sea. It is not fit to drink!"

Fortunately they found a small pond of fresh water that saved them and enabled Sturt to spend six days exploring down the Darling—for so he had named the salty river. By now he had accomplished more than he had set himself to do, and he started back. He knew the secret of those rivers that Oxley had seen losing themselves in reeds and swamps. They did not empty into a sea. They didn't empty anywhere. They simply stopped. And he understood why. This was a country of little rain. The rivers were not fed constantly at their source. They fell rapidly from the mountains into level country, where the great heat dried them up and they ceased to be living streams.

Was the same true of the Darling, this large river with salt springs in its bed? Sturt could see from the water-scoured channel that sometimes furious torrents raged through it. Where did the Darling empty when it was filled with water by the rains? Did it go south to the ocean or did it go west and find a broad inland sea?

Charles Sturt could not get out of his head the idea of that inland sea.

The very next year, when he was tracing the Murrumbidgee River, Sturt found out what happened to the Darling.

He set out with a large party, but swamps made it impossible to follow the river along the banks. He sent back all but seven men. Sturt had brought along a whaleboat in sections. They put it together and also built a small skiff. Then with his companions, five of whom were convicts, he launched himself on the current.

Down the river they went, the current growing faster and carrying them along more and more swiftly till they were going at a fearful speed. From moment to moment they expected to be wrecked on the snags of dead trees that filled the narrow channel. Then all at once they found themselves hurried into a broad and noble river. It was the Murray, Australia's greatest stream, whose upper reaches Hamilton Hume had already found. Sturt followed it south. After a time he caught sight of another stream that joined the Murray. It was the Darling.

All in an instant the key to the whole river system flashed into Sturt's mind. He turned up the Darling to explore it. But some miles up he found a native fishing net stretched across the river. He stopped. For he would not go over it and take the chance of disappointing the people who were depending on the catch for their food that day. Turning, he headed downstream again to see the Murray empty into the ocean.

When he got to the river's mouth, he was dismayed to find that this magnificent stream—which seemed in every way fitted to be a great highway— emptied not directly into the sea but into a lake whose exit was blocked by sand bars and a tremendous surf. Sturt could not hide his disappointment. He had expected to sail around to Sydney, but it was impossible to get out on the sea. Reluctantly he turned to go back the way he had come, for there was no other way to go.

He knew it would be difficult. Yet he didn't begin to foresee how frightful that journey upstream would be. For fifty-eight days the men rowed against the current, often twelve hours and more at a stretch, under a broiling sun. They fell asleep at the oars. They begged Sturt to let them die. One man went insane. But none ever said a word against the leader. They even asked Sturt to take the last of the tea

For weeks the men fought their way upstream.

and sugar for himself. Their salt meat had quickly been exhausted. All they had for food was a little flour and once in a while a bird or fish. More than a thousand miles upstream, it was at last possible to send two of the party for food. After a week they came back with it—just in time to save the rest. Sturt, his eyes damaged by sun and sand, went temporarily blind.

Almost half-heartedly, he reported to the authorities what he had found. It seemed to Captain Sturt that for much of the way the Murray flowed through land that was unfertile or else far from civilization. "The river is misplaced!" he said. He didn't realize that he had opened up to the settlers of Australia a vast and wonderful empire, an area as large as Texas and California put together.

8 *Violence in Van Diemen's Land*

The island we call Tasmania was not always called so. A Dutchman, Abel Tasman, discovered it in 1642. Thinking it was part of the mainland, he named it Van Diemen's Land, after the governor general of the Dutch East Indies. That's how it was known for over two hundred years. But when the people came to hate the convict system so fiercely that they would let no more felons in, they gave the island a new name. For Van Diemen's Land had come to stand for all that is horrible in crime and terrible in punishment.

There was a place halfway up the island's west coast called Macquarie Harbor. It was as wild and gloomy a spot as nature ever made. Its rocky shores were lashed by fierce tempests and drenched almost constantly with rain. Steep heights and gullies choked with scrub looked down upon a foaming sea. Here, on a rocky island that was a half-mile long and a quarter-mile wide, a prison colony for hardened criminals was set up.

"Let it be a warning to evildoers," the governor said.

So Macquarie Harbor became a place of organized terror, where brutal, unjust guards punished men in every cruel way known to them, where pity was unknown and the voice of mercy never heard. A convict passing through the narrow, sand-choked harbor entrance, which was fittingly called Hell's Gates, left all hope behind. He could look forward only to exhausting work, starvation, and flogging—for at Macquarie Harbor even to smile when spoken to was punished by the lash.

Giant trees grew on the hillsides—valuable tim-

The convicts were forced to carry enormous loads.

ber. The wood was heavy. Some of it was so heavy that it would not float. Convicts had to fell and carry this wood down to the sea.

A breakfast of flour and water cooked into a thick gruel started the day. Through the wet, thorny thickets the convicts climbed to the forest. They chopped down the huge, hard trees and lopped off the limbs. Then sixty to eighty men, chained together, would bear a tree on their shoulders down the crooked, rocky path. They swayed under the heavy weight as they struggled over the uneven ground. Soaked to the skin, up and down they went all day. Not till evening would there be a break or would food pass their lips again. After the meal they were too tired to take off their wet clothes. They flung themselves on the floor of their barracks to sleep as they were, while around them rose the nightly "music"—the sound of the lash and the screams of the victims.

There were worse punishments. Even the most hardened thought with dread of the jail with its dark, narrow cells. But worst of all was Pilot Island, the lonely rock reserved for men whom the jail did not subdue. On this tiny island, swept constantly with icy spray whenever the waters were rough, cells had been scooped out of the rock. Here a doomed man would be left for days and weeks to scream himself hoarse with only the sea birds to hear.

Is it any wonder that convicts thought death better than this cruel life? Many a one committed murder so that he might be hanged. Sometimes convicts drew lots to decide who was to be murdered, who would be the murderer, and who the witnesses.

Escape? That was next to impossible. Trackless forests, swift streams, marshes, and 4000-foot heights covered with snow separated Macquarie Harbor from the settled parts of the colony. By sea only a long voyage along the rock-bound coast could bring a man to civilization. Yet convicts escaped. In ten years 112 men dared death and escaped; 62 of them perished. Some who took to the bush were caught and hanged. Some became cannibals before they met their dreadful end. Some were never heard of again. A few made their way to the settled parts and took revenge for the violence that had been done to them. Matthew Brady, who came to be called "Prince of the Bushrangers," was one of these.

Bushranging, which was the new word for banditry, was already in full swing when Matthew Brady took it up. It had started at a time when all the convicts in the settlement were kept busy making roads and putting up buildings. Van Diemen's Land depended on New South Wales for supplies. And when crops on the mainland failed, the colony was faced with famine.

What was to be done? Lieutenant Colonel David Collins, who was in charge, saw no other way than to let the convicts go into the bush and hunt for themselves. He offered twelvepence for every pound of kangaroo meat brought into the government stores. Later he raised it to £1 a pound. So convicts went into the bush to hunt. They found they could get along better on their own and liked it. Some even decided it was more agreeable to stay away altogether.

But, as time went on, convicts were not content to be simply hunters, living on what they shot. Many became bandits. The bushrangers joined in gangs and terrorized the settlers. They robbed people on the roads. They stole cattle, fired houses, plundered, murdered. People in outlying homesteads were forced to live almost as if in the midst of war, with sentinels and loopholes for firing. Bushrangers became so great a menace that the governors were frantic. They threatened. They punished. They offered to forgive and forget if only the bushrangers would come in. But the bandits would not quit robbing and murdering. At one time as many as a hundred armed criminals were spreading terror over the land.

It was in 1824 that handsome Matthew Brady— Gentleman Brady people called him, because he was said to respect women—began to roam the country with his mounted band. As many as twenty-five daredevil followers, all riding fast horses, obeyed his command. The gang burned, plundered, and terrified the settlers. Once Brady led the gang to capture the town of Sorell. He surprised and locked up the soldiers sent against him and let the prisoners out of the jail. When Governor George Arthur offered a reward for his capture, Brady boldly posted a notice saying he was concerned that a person known as George Arthur was at large—and offered twenty gallons of rum to anyone who would deliver that person to him.

Brady's amazing escapes and daring deeds set off a bushranging craze among people who had never committed a crime before. Soldiers deserted and became bushrangers. People with government jobs left them to become bushrangers. The gangs rode stolen horses, hid in distant glens, lived on kangaroo meat or stolen provisions, and dared the government to catch them.

The governor fumed. He wrote letters and gave commands. Finally he offered a huge reward—

three hundred guineas or three hundred acres for the capture of any of twelve members of Brady's band. Any convict who captured one of them would receive a pardon and free passage to England.

Brady had now been bushranging for nearly two years. He was satisfied with the plunder he had gathered and was proposing to his gang that they put a glorious finish to their adventures by escaping from Van Diemen's Land. It was just then that the governor made his proclamation. The tempting reward upset Brady's plans.

Up to this time men had betrayed the government to serve the bandits. Now they betrayed the bandits to get the reward. Thirty-seven bushrangers were turned in. Matthew Brady began to sense that his hour had come. His hide-outs were known. He was constantly harassed and pursued. Separated from his band, wounded in the ankle, without a mount, he found himself at last a fugitive, stumbling along the gullies.

A man named John Batman, who knew the bush well and was famous for his courage, had gone out alone to find the bushranger in the western ranges.

He came upon Brady in a gully. The convict was limping along, leaning on a cut sapling. He seemed to be in great pain. Yet when he caught sight of Batman, the old daredevil spirit returned. Brady's careworn expression changed.

"Stand!" he cried. His gun was at his shoulder, his finger on the trigger. But he did not fire. "Are you a soldier officer?" he asked, and all his hatred of the redcoats was in his voice. He was trying to size up Batman's costume, which had a military look but was not a uniform.

"I'm no soldier, Brady," the other said. "I am John Batman. Surrender, for there is no chance for you."

The bushranger thought a while. Hanging awaited him, he knew, but death had no terror for him now. "You are right, Batman," he said. "My time is come. I will yield to you because you are a brave man."

So ended the career of the most successful convict to escape from Macquarie Harbor. When Matthew Brady had been tried and executed, the colony came to its senses. The "romance" of bushranging was almost over—for the time being.

9 *The Last of the Tasmanians*

In the midst of all this violence in Van Diemen's Land, what was happening to the dark people who for thousands of years had lived there—the Tasmanians?

For some months after the first settlement of white men, the natives did not know that strangers had come into their country. Then one day in the spring of 1803 they found out. A large party of hunters— some three hundred natives with women and children—came by chance on a white settlement. The hunters appeared suddenly on the surrounding hills.

They were driving kangaroos into the valley in order to kill them.

Now it should have been clear to the white men that no harm was intended, for this was quite obviously a hunting party. The presence of the women and children showed that the natives had not come with any warlike intent. And there were the kangaroos. But the governor of the colony was away. The officer left in charge lost his head at the sight of so many natives armed with spears. He gave the command to fire. And some fifty of the people were killed.

This was the beginning. The peaceful, harmless natives had known nothing of violence and cruelty. Now they found themselves suddenly at the mercy of people who thought no more of murdering them than of shooting birds. The convicts had been told to go in the bush and kill kangaroos. They shot the natives as well, stole their women, brained their children, committed every imaginable deed of violence and wrong. Bushrangers in a merry mood would bind natives to trees and use them for target practice.

Convicts working for settlers boasted of how many "black crows" they had destroyed. Some said that white men shot natives to feed to their dogs. And free men acted no better than the convicts. Settlers gave natives presents of poisoned flour. Soldiers treated them to poisoned rum. Townspeople kidnaped their children and, when the unhappy parents pleaded to get them back, answered with brutal jokes.

On every hand the poor, hunted creatures met with cruelty. The white men who had occupied the islands of Bass Strait and made their living by killing seals raided the native tribes to carry off the women as slaves. There was one sealer who stole a dozen women. He put them on different islands to procure kangaroo skins. If they did not do enough work to satisfy him, he would tie them to trees and flog them. If they were stubborn, he killed them.

It was by such acts that the most peaceful people in the world were at last filled with burning hatred of the white men. The dark people of the forest had met the strangers with kindness. But now, whenever they had the chance, they struck. They speared cattle, burned homes, murdered women and children. They were desperate. They determined to drive from their land a race of creatures who had repaid their hospitality with every cruelty known to man. In their rage they were no longer able to tell friend from foe but killed simply because a person was white, as their own people had been killed simply because they were dark.

In 1826 there was so much killing on both sides that the government opened war on the natives. It offered £5 for the capture of every adult and £2 for every child. Men went out in parties to hunt natives. When they couldn't capture one alive, they shot him—and many more were shot than captured. Sometimes in capturing a dozen, thirty would be killed.

The natives carried on war, too. It was a war of wooden spears against guns. But still the white men could not win.

What was to be done?

"This cannot go on," Governor Arthur said. "The natives must be prevented from coming into the settled districts." And he proceeded to carry out the

79

plan. He set up a line of military posts along the edge of the settled districts and issued a proclamation. The natives must immediately go away, the proclamation said, and not come back again on any account. If they wanted to go through to the coast to get shellfish, that was all right, but they must apply for passports.

The natives couldn't read. So they didn't give up their rich, sunny hunting grounds to live among the swamps, scrub, and mountains of the west where there was nothing for them to hunt. Much as it would have pleased the governor to see them depart for that cheerless region of everlasting rain and frost, they stayed right where they were. And they didn't apply for passports to go to collect shellfish.

The war went on. It was murder on one side and murder on the other.

The governor was at his wits' end. Then an idea struck him. He would drive the most troublesome tribes of natives into the southeastern corner of the island and capture the entire lot.

So in the year 1830 great preparations were made.

Eight hundred soldiers and nearly four thousand settlers and police were armed to take part in the drive. They formed in a line that stretched from east to west halfway across the island, with forty-five yards between man and man. Governor Arthur himself took command. Slowly the men in the "Black Line" moved south. After three months they reached the neck of the peninsula. They closed in. And not a single native was there! Except for a woman and a boy who had been caught asleep some time before, all had slipped through the line. More than £20,000 had been spent—and the total result was one woman and a boy.

A year passed. Then the governor got another chance.

The season of swans' eggs was approaching. This was a favorite food of the native people, and they made a holiday of the yearly gathering of the eggs on Schouten Peninsula. Many tribes came together then, family reunions took place, and there was great rejoicing. The neck of the peninsula where the swans nested was only a mile wide. Would it not be the simplest thing in the world to draw a cordon across it, cut off the people's retreat, and capture them all at leisure?

So again troops, settlers, and police came together. They were confident of success because a large party of natives had been seen moving stealthily toward the peninsula. The Europeans drew up across the neck and built great fires. The plan was for some to guard the entrance with dogs and arms while others went in to seize or kill the egg-gatherers.

When the natives saw the fires and heard the barking of the dogs, they understood that they were trapped. Only daring could save them now. They waited for a favorable opportunity and saw it in a moonless night. They crept as close to the fires as they dared. Then, with a leap and a cry, each one dashed by the fires and dogs and guards and reached the forest.

About this time a small, red-haired man stepped forward with a different kind of plan.

"Let me go into the bush unarmed," he said, "and talk to the natives and try to get them to surrender.

If I can get them to listen to me, I will explain to them that the Europeans wish only to better their condition."

The man who made this bold proposal was George Augustus Robinson, of the town of Hobart. He was a bricklayer by trade and a strong Methodist by religion. He had a deep feeling for the natives and was heartsick over the way they were being treated. He had learned their language, had made friends among the natives who strayed around Hobart Town, and had brought them to his house. When the captives taken in the Black War had been placed on Bruni Island, he had been put in charge. The natives were not happy with their rations of bread and potatoes. "No good this place," they complained. "Bad place. No egg, no kangaroo. No like. All die." Still it was better for them to be there than to be killed off, Robinson thought. He was convinced it was his mission to go and bring in the rest of the people.

Hardly anybody besides himself had any faith in his plan. "You are a mad enthusiast," someone said.

"I wouldn't give a fig for a man who enters upon anything important unless he has enthusiasm," Rob-

83

inson retorted. And he went out into the bush—
unarmed but not alone. Several white men went with
him. He depended much more, however, on some
dozen or so of his native friends from Bruni, who
went along to persuade their friends and relatives to
yield. And most of all he relied on Truganina. Truganina was a native woman devoted to Robinson.
She was beautiful, wise in counsel, full of devices,
and very brave. She loved adventure, and on several
occasions she was to save Robinson's life.

The natives dashed past their pursuers.

Decorated with gaudy ribbons to catch the eyes of natives in the bush, the women went ahead to make contact with the tribes. They distributed trinkets. But it was not these that won the natives over. The women appealed to the strong family feeling of the people. This one had a brother or sister in a neighboring tribe, that one had a father or mother. The women sought to unite families and to save their loved ones from the danger of war. At the right moment Robinson would advance. He would try to persuade the people that it was better for them to surrender than to go into the settled areas and carry on the war.

"If you go there, you get killed," he would say. "If you come with me, you will get plenty of food."

So he talked to them, and little by little he got them to yield. By 1831 Robinson and his assistants had won over sixteen tribes. Even the dreaded Big River tribe, which Governor Arthur had wanted so much to capture inside his "Black Line," surrendered. They yielded to Robinson, not as prisoners but as friends. The Big River tribe were not many now—sixteen men, nine women, and one child.

When Robinson brought them in, the whole population of Hobart turned out to see the procession. First came Robinson with his white companions. Then came his fourteen native followers. Then came the twenty-six wilder people of the forest, the men carrying their long spears. The governor was deeply moved, and women wept.

Afterward Robinson returned to the bush, going farther and farther west. He crossed rivers and mountains in the dead of winter. Once for seven days his party went through snow that was often up to their waists. In the country where desperate fugitives from Macquarie Harbor perished, he and his faithful assistants survived. At the end of 1834 they took in their last group—four women, a man, and three boys. This party had long wanted to surrender and join their relatives. They had even ventured in sight of a settler's hut. But a shot had warned them that they had better stay in the inhospitable mountains. Now as they saw Robinson's assistants coming, they ran forward and embraced them in a moving manner.

They were all in now. Except for a single family in the far north, whom a sealer would bring in in

1842, not one of the thousands who had once roamed the land remained at liberty to hunt the kangaroo. Less than three hundred of the entire race were left alive. These few were taken to a bleak island in Bass Strait; their children were taken from them and put in an orphan asylum, while they themselves were left to pine away in sight of their once happy home.

In captivity, the Australian koala bear sulks and dies. Just so the Tasmanians drooped and died. They died of homesickness.

Truganina was the last to go. She died in 1876. She had been born in the year the first settlers came to Van Diemen's Land. In her lifetime her whole race vanished.

"Bury me behind the mountains," she pleaded on her deathbed, recalling the wonderful adventures she had lived through by Robinson's side. But her wish was not granted. In the interests of science her skeleton was preserved. It stands today in the museum at Hobart.

10 *Squatters on the Land*

Big, jolly John Batman, his curly black hair tumbling over his forehead, stormed into Fawkner's Inn at Launceston, Van Diemen's Land. The year was 1835, nine years after his capture of Matthew Brady. "Look here, you fellows!" he roared. "I'm the biggest landowner in the world!"

As he spoke, he unrolled a parchment scroll and spread it out on the bar. "Here's my treaty with the Dutigallas," he said. "Lawyer friend of mine drew it up."

Everybody crowded around. It was a treaty, right enough, with all the fancy language a treaty should have: "We do grant, enfeoff, and confirm . . ." And there were the chiefs' signatures—eight wavy lines with the names of the chiefs written in neatly beside them—Cooloolock, Bungarie, Yanyan, Moowhip, Mommarmalar, and Jaga-Jaga, which was down three times. "They're three brothers," Batman explained. "All of them have the same name."

John Batman was proud of his bargain. He had "bought" from the native Dutigallas of the Port Phillip region—which was on the mainland, just across Bass Strait—600,000 acres of land. A piece of territory measuring nearly a thousand square miles was his. In exchange for it he had given 20 pairs of blankets, 30 knives, 12 tomahawks, 10 mirrors, 12 pairs of scissors, 50 handkerchiefs, 12 red shirts, 4 flannel jackets, 4 suits of clothes, and 50 pounds of flour. It was not much of a price for a stretch of land three times the size of the city of New York. But it was the first time, John Batman reflected, that anyone had thought of paying the natives anything at all.

"Wonderful grazing country," he said enthusiastically. "Plenty of water. And there's a spot just right for a village." He was thinking of the place where the city of Melbourne would one day rise.

A good many people from Van Diemen's Land took Batman at his word. They ferried their sheep and bullocks over to the fine pastures across the way and squatted on the land. They just laughed when Batman said they were trespassing on the property of the Port Phillip Association. They chopped down trees and cleared land. Batman had to make the best of it, for he had no way of defending the rights of the company he had formed. But anyway there was land enough. They would all get along.

In time more squatters came to join them. Two years later, 100,000 sheep were grazing in what would one day be the colony of Victoria. And now the Dutigallas began to comprehend the meaning of Batman's treaty.

John Batman told everybody that the chiefs had understood perfectly what they were doing, and he truly believed it himself. Hadn't they gone with him to the boundaries of the land and themselves marked the trees at the corners? Then each had given him a chunk of earth by way of putting him in possession. Surely they couldn't suppose he had given them all those blankets and other things for nothing?

But Batman deceived himself. The Australian natives had no idea what "selling" land meant. They had no notion that an individual could "own" land. The land was simply there. They believed it belonged to all, just as the air and the sea and the kangaroos and the shellfish belonged to all.

The natives could no longer feed themselves. The sheep grazed on the land where they had once hunted. The plant food on which they had depended was destroyed. Disturbed by the loud report of the settlers' guns, the wild fowl had left the creeks. The hungry people were bewildered. Where could they go? The inland tribes would not let the Dutigallas occupy their territory.

The natives were dying of disease and idleness and starvation. They could not foresee that, fifty years after making the treaty with Batman, only a few dozen of them would be left out of the thousands that had lived in the Port Phillip district. But they felt themselves to be strangers in their own land. According to the ancient customs, any food in sight must be shared by the entire tribe; but now they were forbidden to kill a single one of the white man's sheep and cattle. The natives did kill them—on the sly at first. Then they killed for spite. At last their pent-up rage burst forth and they murdered two white men.

The authorities in Sydney heard about it. They were less concerned about the murders than about the fact that white men had taken possession of land that belonged to the crown. Batman's treaty was a joke, of course: the land was the queen's. "You are invaders," the authorities said. "You have no more right to graze your sheep there than on Her Majesty's lawn at Windsor Park. Anybody found holding land without a license will be dealt with as a trespasser."

But these were just words. The authorities sent a party representing the governor to form a new settlement and attempt to control the squatters. But there was little that the government could really do about them. They were there and they were going to stay. More were on the way. They were coming overland from Sydney, driving their herds of cattle.

Governor Bourke protested. "Settlers must stay within the nineteen counties around Sydney, for I cannot give them protection beyond," he said. He might as well have forbidden the tides to rise on the beach. Who wanted protection? The squatters would protect themselves. What they wanted was pasture, miles of pasture if they could get it. Loading their household goods on creaking wagons, the land-hungry pioneers pushed out to find broad, grassy plains for their cattle and sheep.

They raced to get the best lands. A man would ride ahead of his flocks to find good, unoccupied land. He might come to initials cut in a tree that would show him the land was already taken. Or he might see a line plowed in the earth. Perhaps a squatter would tell him where there was a good piece of unoccupied land. When the new man found a place he liked, he would climb a hill and shout: "All I see, I claim!" Then he would squat on the land—perhaps hundreds of acres.

The pioneers pushed on to find good land.

What cared he for the governor's threats? He was there. The land was his. He would not be able to get title, the governor said? Let the authorities just try to get him off the land.

11 *Toward the Heart of the Continent*

After Captain Sturt's exploration of the Darling and
Murray rivers, he wished some day to get to the very
center of Australia. But many years passed before
he set out to do it. In the meantime the southern
land which he had opened up became the most
promising part of the continent. The plains of South
Australia and its rich, lovely valleys were studded
with cottages and wheat fields. The Murray had become the high road to connect east and south. On
the southern coast, the city of Adelaide had sprung
up.

In 1844 Charles Sturt, married and settled down,

97

was himself a leading citizen of Adelaide. He had come overland, driving three hundred cattle to the fine new pasture lands. But now he had given up farming. He held an official post, but he was not happy in it. When he was asked to learn what lay in the center of Australia, he eagerly made ready to go. He had high expectations of what he would find. For he had watched the birds migrating northward and had thought, "If the birds fly to the interior, it must be a fertile place." He meant to follow their route.

His party was made up of eighteen men. It included John McDouall Stuart, a young fellow who would one day make great expeditions of his own, but who was now just learning. The whole town of Adelaide turned out to see the expedition start. The horses, the bullocks hauling carts, and the two hundred sheep being driven along for food made quite a sight. Captain Sturt followed the Murray and the Darling north, and at the end of January 1845 made camp on the shore of a little lake.

The heat was terrific. For three months the temperature averaged 103 degrees in the shade. It kept the men tied to their base, for they dared not leave the water. In vain Sturt looked for some trail to take them farther, but in no direction could he find a single life-giving puddle.

Six months passed. The precious lake water sank lower and lower. One man died. Most of the men were sick with scurvy. The heat was so intense that their flour dried up, their hair stopped growing, their fingernails became brittle. The hot sands burned the skin off the dogs' feet.

Then the rain came. "This is my one chance," Sturt thought. He sent back all but four men. Taking four horses, a light cart, and fifteen weeks' provisions, he made a dash for the heart of the continent.

They pushed ahead, grateful for every drop of water and every blade of grass. The puddles were beginning to dry up when they came out on a boundless flat plain, littered with great sand-rounded pebbles. Sturt had never seen anything like this Stony Desert. He was looking for a sea. He did not realize that he was struggling over the remains of one. Ages ago on this spot a sea had rolled. It had dried, its bed had cracked in the heat, and these strange stones had formed.

For fifty miles Sturt struggled across the Stony Desert. But now there spread before him a heart-breaking sight. Climbing to the top of a bare, sandy ridge, he saw a whole succession of ridges just like it, fifty to one hundred feet high, stretching unbroken to the horizon. They were like the waves of a sea.

Sturt sat with his head in his hands. His disappointment was almost more than he could bear. There wasn't a drop of water or a blade of grass ahead, and behind him the water holes were drying up.

"No man has a greater claim than I to explore Central Australia!" he thought bitterly. "It is my right to see what lies at the heart of the continent!" He could not do it.

Sadly he gave the order to turn back. He and his companions made all the haste they could, and in eight weeks they got back to the base. All the party were ill, but Sturt more so than any. Had not friendly natives cared for him and made him

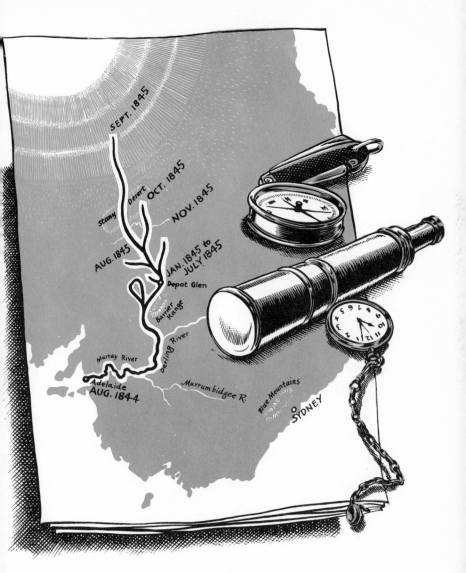

From Adelaide, Captain Sturt explored far inland.

THE STORY OF AUSTRALIA

eat berries to cure his scurvy, he would have died.

The heat was terrible. A thermometer that Sturt put in a sheltered place burst the bulb when the mercury rose above 127 degrees. The ground was so hot that matches falling on it were ignited. All the grass was gone from near the camp and the natives warned Sturt that the water in Flood Creek was disappearing. The last retreat began. Sturt made a dash for the creek and launched the boat he had brought. How vain had been his dream that it "would plow the waters of a central sea"!

Toward the end of the journey, Sturt was again able to ride. But as he approached Adelaide, two gentlemen in a carriage met him and brought him in triumph to the town. The rest of the party came in a few days later—gaunt, their faces hidden in unkempt hair, their skin burned almost the color of the natives. The horses were living skeletons.

As he thought the adventure over, Charles Sturt felt that all the terrible sufferings had been for naught. He had not found any good country, he had not found an inland sea, he had not reached the center of the continent.

But others felt differently. He had mapped unknown country. He had shown the way to the interior. John McDouall Stuart proved it when on his way north in 1860 he fulfilled Captain Sturt's ambition by placing the Union Jack on a peak in the very center of Australia. As was only right, he called the peak Central Mount Sturt.

12 Caroline Chisholm

and the New Australians

Governor Gipps had something distasteful to go through. He had received a letter from a Mrs. Caroline Chisholm, who wanted to see him about a house for unemployed immigrant girls.

"She must be some charity crank," he said to his wife. "I can imagine her—an old lady in a white cap and colored spectacles who will talk to me about my soul."

"My dear," his wife said, "you have to see her nevertheless."

So the governor did. He was very much surprised

when his visitor turned out to be a handsome young woman. He was even more amazed when she argued with him as though she thought her reasons and her experience were every bit as good as his own. The governor wasn't used to this sort of thing. He hemmed and hawed and felt embarrassed. But he was firm: he could not let her have a penny of government money. "The best I can do for you is to let you use the old empty barracks down near the docks," he said. "Only, mind you, it must not cost the government a thing." And he dismissed the lady.

What was it all about? Why did immigrant girls need a home? And who was this Caroline Chisholm who had braved the governor for their sake?

Unemployed immigrant girls were something new in Australia. Up to now there had not been people enough to do all the work. The new problem had started after 1831, when England began to help poor people to pay their passage out to Australia. New machines in the factories had cut down the need for workers, and English cities were filled with the unemployed. Thousands dreamed of going out to Australia, where they expected to get a better chance to make a living. Perhaps they might some day even have a bit of land of their own!

Many uprooted themselves gladly when given the chance. Others needed persuasion to leave home and family and friends. And the ship owners saw to it that they got it. Ship companies sent out agents to try to get people to emigrate, paying a "bounty" or commission on each passenger the agents brought in. For the greedy ship owners saw a chance to make a handsome profit out of carrying the immigrants. Just pack them in like sheep and feed them next to nothing—that was the idea!

Conditions on the overcrowded sailing vessels were frightful. Passengers had to do their own cooking, and the food handed out to them was both scanty and bad. Fevers and illness of all sorts broke out. On one ship over a hundred people died during the voyage. When after half a year at sea the poor, ill-used immigrants finally landed in the strange country, they were worn out and generally penniless. They would start looking for work and would find that in Sydney there was no work for them to do.

For immigrants who had come before them and gone out to work on the farms had found they couldn't stand convict wages and convict conditions. They had come back to the city. Hundreds tramped the streets in despair, and nobody seemed to care if they lived or died.

Many of the immigrants were girls who had come alone and had neither fathers nor brothers nor husbands to protect them. A girl would come out in the hope of getting a place as dairymaid or servant on a farm. She didn't know how to get such a job, for there was no employment office. She couldn't just set off into the bush along a bullock track. Since she had no money, she slept in a cave in the Rocks, which was the worst part of Sydney. In the daytime she hung around taverns, hoping that someone would give her a loaf of bread.

One Sunday morning Caroline Chisholm, the wife of an army captain and the mother of three children, was going to church when she saw a girl leap into Sydney Harbor. The girl was Flora McDonald, a penniless immigrant seeking to end her life. Mrs. Chisholm rescued her, found lodgings for her, and learned from her lips what immigrant girls were up against. And as she listened, it seemed to Caroline Chisholm that she heard a call: "Do not shut your eyes to the misery of these unfortunates."

Afterward people could not understand how Mrs. Chisholm could undertake such daring things for the sake of strangers. But to Caroline Chisholm it all seemed natural. For she had early learned to feel and act for people outside the family circle. When she was a little girl on an English farm, her father had taken in a wounded soldier and cared for him. It had been a great object lesson to her. Later, when she understood about emigration, her favorite doll play had been helping families to settle in distant lands. She would put a family of dolls in a big china basin and send them floating off to build a colony over the sea. Now Caroline Chisholm was acting out her childhood dream.

When the next ship arrived, she was at the dock to meet it. Sixty immigrant girls had an average of only a few pennies each in their pockets. She found lodgings for them all, fed them, collected clothes for them, got them jobs. But as more ships came in, she found that her home in Windsor, which was a day's journey out of Sydney, was too far from the docks. It was then that she asked Governor Gipps to help her.

That same night Caroline Chisholm, with her own small baby, moved into the barracks the governor had offered her. The place was a wretched slab hut, without even a stove to cook on. If a prisoner employed in the printing office next door had not been kind enough to bring her some hot water, she could not have had even a cup of tea. She went to bed. But she had scarcely put out her candle when a fearful racket broke out. She thought that dogs must be in the room. She lit the candle again—and saw rats coming from all directions. At one time she counted thirteen. She sat on her bed watching them.

"I'm getting a fever," she thought. "I shall be ill before morning."

When three rats came down from the roof onto her shoulders, she pulled herself together and took action. "It would be too bad to be defeated by rats," she told herself. She had two loaves of bread and some butter. She cut the whole into slices, set them in the middle of the room, and put a dish of water conveniently near. Then with a light by her side she sat on her bed till four in the morning, reading a book and watching the rats eat the bread.

In this unsavory place Caroline Chisholm settled down, made a home for her girls, and ran an employment agency. She had talked everything over with her husband, who had agreed that this was something she must do. A nurse had been hired to take care of their children, but the mother kept in touch with them so well and so lovingly that in after years not one had a reproach to make.

Gifts of money and clothing began to come in and—more precious—letters about jobs that were open on back-country farms. The girls were frightened. They didn't dare take a long journey into the bush. They had heard about bushrangers and poisonous snakes and murderous natives.

"Nonsense," Mrs. Chisholm said. "I will take you myself."

She chartered a river steamer. At every landing farmers were waiting. But before she let them take the girls, each man had to sign a contract that he would offer good wages and fair treatment.

After that first journey Caroline Chisholm went by land. She would ride in front on a horse, and the girls would follow, some riding in a cart, some walking and changing places with the riders from time to time. It became a famous sight on the bullock tracks of New South Wales to see Mrs. Chisholm leading her girls to jobs and homes in the "outback."

"She's a second Moses," people said, "a Moses in bonnet and shawl, leading her people to the Promised Land." Often innkeepers would feed her party for nothing. Wagon drivers would give the girls a ride.

Her vigor and spirit carried her even through such hardships as crossing the Blue Mountains with 150 girls. Men and whole families turned to her, and once she journeyed three hundred miles to settle a single family. During her six years in Sydney she obtained jobs for more than eleven thousand people!

There seemed to be no limit to the energy and daring Caroline Chisholm was putting into her one-

111

Caroline Chisholm found jobs and homes for thousands.

woman revolution for the better treatment of immigrants. She struck at the greedy ship owners, exposing the terrible conditions on the ships, particularly the way the young girls were treated. She brought a case into court, and the captain and doctor of one ship were punished for their handling of passengers. She wrote pamphlets about life in Australia so that immigrants would know truly what they were facing. But perhaps her greatest work was in bringing families together. She went herself to England. She found and sent to Australia hundreds of children whom their parents had been persuaded to leave behind, often in English poorhouses, where they had lived miserably for years. She hunted out and sent over wives who had given up hope of seeing their husbands again.

By this time people of wealth and influence had become interested in the work of this heroic woman. They lent her their support. A society was formed, and seven ships were chartered to take deserving families to New South Wales under a co-operative plan. Although Mrs. Chisholm's health was failing now, she turned the energy of her last years to securing homestead land for her immigrant friends.

Caroline Chisholm saw no greatness in what she had done—only hard work, wearisome journeys, thousands of interviews, tens of thousands of letters. But recognition was hers in plenty. People spoke of her as the greatest Australian woman. And a distinguished French writer called her the "only saint" in Australia.

13 *Gold Rush in the Island Continent*

Gold! Gold had been found in California!

Everybody in Sydney was talking of fortunes to be picked off the ground. And people were not just talking, but sailing off to California in droves. Among the gold hunters from Sydney were many ex-convicts. They could well be spared; California would find them giving her plenty of trouble. But what about men who had just immigrated to Australia? Government funds had been spent to help them cross the ocean. But they no sooner landed and found that the work was hard than they skipped off to California! The land was being emptied. Ah, what a fine thing it would be if gold were discovered in Australia! Then there would be a rush in instead of a rush out. England could stop sending over convicts and the immigrants would stay.

This was a new way of looking at things. For there had been several hints of gold on the continent, and always the government had wanted the matter kept quiet. With so many convicts around, it was thought, a gold rush would be a dangerous thing. In 1841 a minister who was also an amateur geologist discovered a bit of gold in a creek near Bathurst, about a hundred miles west of Sydney. When he showed it to Governor Gipps, the governor said, "Put it away, Mr. Clarke, or we shall all have our throats cut."

Among those who went off to seek a fortune on America's west coast was Edward Hargraves, a young man from that very same Bathurst area. Hargraves didn't find many gold nuggets in California. But one day, as he sat looking around him despondently, he suddenly realized that the landscape where the most gold had been found looked strangely like the scenery around his home in New South Wales.

He hurried back by the first ship. In February

1851 he was on his way into his native hills, and with him were three friends whom he had persuaded to go gold-hunting too. They started panning gravel from a creek bed, swirling the dirt in a tin dish. At the very first wash, a little gold was left in the dish. As pan after pan showed gold, the men's excitement grew. They would be rich, they would be famous! "I shall be a baronet," Hargraves said to his friends. "You will be knighted. The horse I ride to carry the news will be stuffed, put in a glass case, and sent to the British Museum."

He left his friends working and went off to tell the news to the Colonial Secretary in Sydney. There was bound to be a prize for the discovery of gold; £500 would be a neat sum. In the end, Edward Hargraves got £12,381 plus £250 a year for the rest of his life.

The news spread like a bush fire. People dropped whatever they were doing and headed for Hargraves' diggings. But this was only the start. Soon a bigger find was made in the Bathurst area. Sydney was deserted. Sailors left their ships. Schools shut their doors as the teachers headed for the hills. Shops were closed as, with shovels over their shoulders, the clerks tramped off to the mines. In the country-side, shepherds abandoned their flocks, farmers left their crops unharvested.

Men rode horses, donkeys, or any animals they could find. Many walked, pushing their camp out-fits along in wheelbarrows. Their feet beat out new trails to distant gullies, and their tents of tattered canvas fluttered on a dozen hillsides.

The region of gold strikes grew wider. A native shepherd showed his master a "big feller yellow stone" he had found. It turned out to contain about a hundred pounds of pure gold. Men hurried to the site.

Diggers did not come to Bathurst from Sydney alone. They came all the way from Melbourne, four hundred miles away in Victoria. This region had just won the right to be a separate colony, and the au-thorities were worried about so many people drift-ing off to New South Wales. If only gold could be found in Victoria! Some wealthy men offered a prize to anyone who would discover gold near Melbourne.

Prospectors went out. And at once they began striking rich gold. Gravel on the upper Yarra River sparkled with grains of gold. In August 1851 the fabulous Ballarat fields were struck. Four months later those at Bendigo were found. The golden stream had turned into a flood. By the end of 1851, gold worth over £1,000,000 had been taken out.

Ballarat and Bendigo—glittering names! Everything that had been found in Bathurst paled by comparison. Nothing like the Victoria mines had been seen in the world before. Nothing like them has been seen since. A Ballarat digger at the bottom of a hole only five feet deep saw gold so thickly sprinkled that "it looked like a jeweler's shop." The "Welcome Stranger" nugget, biggest in history, weighed 142 pounds and was worth over £10,000.

Luckiest of all were two young boys. One day in 1855, they came with bags on their backs to a crushing mill near Bendigo. They got permission to use the mortar and pestle in the work tent, but waited till the men had gone to lunch. Then they put their dirty-looking quartz rocks in the mortar and began pounding. Flakes of shining gold fell away. The boys jumped when they saw that the mill owner was watching them.

"Father and mother are on the diggings," the elder one said in answer to the man's questions. "We went looking ourselves and found a little quartz reef with lots of gold. We brought this much around by the back gully. Is it worth aught?"

The mill owner weighed their take. "Worth £624, I figure. You want cash?"

"Thanks, no." They put the gold in their bags and slipped off. Ten days later they were back. This time an older lad was pushing along a wheelbarrow for them. It was loaded with ore. Most of the men in the camp gathered around to watch the boys as they freed the gold from the quartz. Even the hardened gold hunters were dazzled by the richness of the rocks.

"Give you £1200 for the ore," offered one bearded watcher.

"Thanks, sir, no."

"Father and mother know about it?"

"Not yet."

Some rivers sparkled with gold.

"Where did ye say this came from?"

"Didn't say."

Again the boys disappeared. But the secret could not be kept forever. The next time they came they were followed back to Victoria Hill, and one of the great Bendigo rushes began. The boys had discovered the richest quartz lode in the world. A German bought their claim and made £40,000 from it.

Melbourne was now more deserted than Sydney, but news of strikes like this brought gold-thirsty men to Victoria from all over the world. From Norway to China echoed the call: "Gold in Australia! Come and get your share!" In sight of Melbourne, sailors would jump overboard, swim ashore, and head for the diggings. A hundred thousand men poured through the city in less than a year.

Gold brought together people who were worlds apart in every sense. An escaped convict from Van Diemen's Land might work on his little claim side by side with a future prime minister of England. An Irishman without a grade-school education might become the partner of a German aristocrat. All were united by their common search for gold.

14 *Battle at the Eureka Stockade*

In the 1850's gold tripled the population of Australia.

The government officials said: "We have to spend a lot more money now to build roads and keep order. Why shouldn't the diggers pay for it? Let each one give a certain amount each month for a license to dig."

At first the fee was 30 shillings a month. Then it was doubled. In the beginning, when gold was plentiful and the yellow metal lay near the surface, the tax was not a great hardship. But later on, when the gold ran thin and many miners dug and dug for months without earning a penny, the license fee became a sore point with them. The worst of it was that the police who collected the fee made a grim game of it. These police were supposed to protect the miners, but they behaved so that the diggers had good reason to regard them as enemies.

A cry of "Joe! Joe!" echoing up the pitted hillside was the signal that police were making a raid. A burly officer would demand that the miner climb up from his muddy underground workings and produce a paper to show that he had paid his monthly tax. Sometimes a bullying policeman would make a man show his paper four or five times in one day, just for the satisfaction of seeing him climb out of his hole at command. In the deeper pits, diggers had water to contend with and frequently were obliged to change their clothes. Sometimes when they did that, they would forget and leave their licenses behind. That made no difference to the police. If a man didn't have his license with him, whatever the reason, the police would chase him all over the diggings and drag him to a pen. First he would be chained to a log for hours in the sun and then

124

herded to town, where he would be heavily fined or imprisoned for breaking the law.

The miners finally blazed out in open rebellion. The occasion of it was a murder.

A digger was killed in a scuffle outside a shanty called the Eureka Hotel. The man who ran this "hotel" was one James Bentley, a former convict from Van Diemen's Land. The diggers were sure he had killed their comrade, but Bentley was a friend of the judge, and the judge set him free. The miners were enraged. Ten thousand gathered outside the Eureka Hotel to protest. And when police tried to break up the crowd, the shanty was burned to the ground. Later the innkeeper was tried again and convicted, but in the meantime three miners, picked at random, were arrested for the burning of the hotel.

The aroused diggers now found a leader in Peter Lalor.

He was a man of fine family, one of the eighteen sons of Patrick Lalor, an Irish member of the British Parliament. At this time Peter was twenty-seven years old. Over six feet tall, manly, earnest, trained as a civil engineer, he was in every way fitted to lead his fellow miners, whom he respected and felt to be badly treated. The murdered digger had been his friend. Peter regarded it as his plain duty to see that justice was done.

When the three diggers were arrested for the burning of the Eureka Hotel, a committee of miners went to plead with the government. They got nowhere. Clearly action was called for. On November 29, 1854, ten thousand diggers met on Bakery Hill. They made a bonfire of their hated licenses and signed up as members of the recently founded Ballarat Reform League. Peter Lalor was one of the speakers. The League asked an end to the licenses. And it demanded that every man in Victoria be allowed the vote.

The government lost no time in striking back. The very next day a troop of mounted and foot police held another hunt for diggers. Eight men were arrested and numbers of men on both sides were wounded.

The miners were outraged. They flocked from all directions to Bakery Hill, where they found Peter

Lalor standing with a rifle in his hands and his friends by his side. One of these was Carboni Raffaelo, a fiery Italian who in his own country had done his bit fighting against tyranny.

Lalor marshaled the men two abreast, and they marched up a hill to the old Eureka claim, where they elected him commander in chief. He made a brief speech, promising to be courageous and never to betray the cause. He and his lieutenants proclaimed the "Republic of Victoria." Then the miners hoisted their banner to the top of an eighty-foot pole. It showed the silver stars of the Southern Cross on a pale blue ground. Everybody was deeply moved. "We swear by the Southern Cross," they repeated solemnly, "to stand truly by each other and fight to defend our rights and liberties."

Gathering logs and slabs, they enclosed an acre of ground. It was a flimsy stockade, more something to keep the men together than a place of defense. But they fully intended to keep their oath. So they drilled with poles and pitchforks and the few guns they had. However, it didn't look as if any danger was near, and some of the miners drifted back to their claims. On Saturday night only about two hundred men passed the night behind the stockade.

Then in the gray dawn a bugle outside sounded the alarm: "Commence firing."

They were under attack!

The miners sprang to their feet and looked beyond the stockade. Three hundred yards away was a force of 276 soldiers and police, more than half of them on horseback. As the miners frantically fired into their midst, the troops came over the stockade with bayonets fixed.

Raffaelo fought like a tiger, and Peter Lalor was in the forefront, but it was all over in a few moments. Some of the miners, unused to battle, fled into the gullies. Of the rest, over a hundred were taken prisoner. Fourteen were killed—some after they had asked for mercy. The police, who were mad for revenge, would give no quarter. Ten of the rebels died later of their wounds. Of the attacking force, one was killed and four fatally wounded.

In the very first attack, Lalor had been twice hit. One musket ball wounded him in the side. Another shattered his left shoulder. Faint with loss of blood,

The soldiers and police advanced upon the rebels.

he fell. A friend covered him over with slabs, and, face down in the dust, he escaped the bayonets in the massacre that followed. Later his friends disguised him, put him on a horse, and helped him hide in the bush till nightfall. Although £200 was offered for information leading to his arrest, not one of the miners betrayed him.

The rebellion was over. The prisoners were hauled off to jail, and there they sat for four months, worrying about what was happening to their wives and children. The authorities had made up their minds to "crush the scoundrels." They selected thirteen, including Raffaelo, to be put on trial, meaning to make an example of them.

But the people of Melbourne, disgusted with the way the police had behaved, were solidly behind the miners. So the government was discredited by the affair. The thirteen miners were acquitted, the hated license fee was abolished—and within a year every man in Victoria had the vote.

But the miners' rebellion had much more meaning than this. Eureka Stockade was Australia's Bunker Hill. It was a first blow for freedom. For the first

130

time men in that land banded together to fight against tyranny.

Peter Lalor lost his arm as a result of that fight, but for the rest of his life he drew deep strength from that experience. A great career opened up for him in politics. For thirty-two years he was a Member of Parliament in Victoria, and for seven years he was Speaker of the House. Yet in time of need his mind always went back to the Eureka Stockade. It was of that gray dawn he was thinking when almost with his last breath, he said, "It is sweet and pleasant to die for one's country, but it is sweeter to live and see the principles for which you have risked your life triumphant."

15 *Cobb & Co.*

Freeman Cobb was a shrewd Yankee who came from America to Ballarat in the "golden fifties." Like thousands of others, he had been lured by the chance of making a fortune digging. But he hit on a surer and pleasanter way of making money: he would provide the diggers with a comfortable means of travel. Victoria did not as yet have a single railroad. The coaches of those days were slow, creaking, jolting vehicles that made no more than ten to twenty miles in a day. Here was a chance that others had overlooked. Why, there wasn't a miner who didn't have to go to Melbourne every so often!

So with three other Americans, who also hadn't grown rich digging, he started Cobb & Co. They sent all the way to Connecticut for coaches that would take the worst jolting out of travel. They paid $1000 apiece, and the coaches were worth it. They were hung on leather springs, which was something new for Australia. They were so much better than the clumsy affairs already on the roads that before long Cobb & Co. had all the business in Victoria to themselves.

James Rutherford of New York joined the firm. He was a man of superb ideas, a showman, a fellow who might well have run a circus. He, too, had come to Victoria to dig gold. But he hadn't had much luck and had gone into other ventures. He traveled up and down the east coast buying and selling horses, stock, timber. When Cobb & Co. asked him to be their manager, James Rutherford eagerly agreed. The job appealed to his imagination.

Rutherford would have nothing but the best, and it was always the showy best. Style—that was what he liked. He brought in crack drivers from America, men who had had experience with famous coaching

133

firms such as Wells Fargo. He paid them fabulous wages—as much as £1000 a year—and he had them teach local men so that the firm would be able to expand.

He stocked up with the best and most beautiful matching horses that money could buy. It was like looking at a bit of circus parade to see a Cobb & Co. coach on its way. For years the most exciting sight in Melbourne was the daily departure of the Ballarat

Cobb & Co. coaches carried passengers, mail, and gold.

coaches, each drawn by twelve snow-white horses.
A person couldn't help feeling grand and important
when he rode in a coach like that.

But the greatest spectacle on the roads was the
Leviathan coach that ran between Castlemaine and
Kyneton. The great "Leviathan," carrying seventy-
five passengers, was drawn by a team of twenty-two
matched gray horses. Each horse was groomed to
the last hair. Gay blue rosettes decorated the polished harness. The saddle cloths were blue. The
mountings were silver. It was a thrill to see the coach
get on the way—the company's flag flying, the guard
blowing his horn, the four postilions riding like
jockeys forward, and the proud coachman with reins
and whip in his hands displaying a magnificent air
of confidence.

After a time, most of the drivers were Australians.
They were celebrities, discussed the way movie stars
are today. "Silent Bob" was famous for his dislike of
conversation. "What plant is that growing in the
field?" a passenger asked him one day. Silent Bob
didn't answer. A week later, when the same man

was on his way home, the driver snarled at him, "Lucerne, I tell yer!" The story went up and down the land.

Every driver had something special about him, and people loved to give them nicknames. "Cabbage-Tree Ned" they called one because of the woven palm-leaf hat he wore. Ned was the most famous of all the coachmen, and to him was given the proud honor of driving the coach, drawn by twelve gray horses, that bore the first English cricket team to visit Australia. But all the drivers were magical figures. Speeding through the bush, over gullies and creeks and flats, crossing flooded rivers, defying bushrangers, taking chances by day and night, Cobb & Co.'s drivers captured the imagination.

James Rutherford was having a wonderful time. When Freeman Cobb went back to the United States in 1859, Rutherford bought out the firm. Running the coach service did more than satisfy his love of showmanship. It gave him the feeling of being at the heart of the country's life. Cobb & Co. carried the mail to the countryside. It brought news and

137

visitors from afar. It took happy people to town and sick people to the doctor. And it carried the precious gold from the mines to the banks in town.

Steadily Rutherford extended his service toward the north. The news that Cobb & Co. was going north into New South Wales went ahead. When the procession crossed the border, crowds turned out to welcome it in every town. It was something to see 103 dashing horses, ten gaily painted coaches, and three feeder wagons, one drawn by six matching grays, another by six roans, another by six bays.

When James Rutherford had put every other coach in New South Wales out of business, he pushed still farther north, crossing the border into Queensland. And still the number of horses and coaches and drivers grew. By 1870 Cobb & Co. were harnessing 6000 horses a day. The coaches were traveling 28,000 miles a week. The drivers were being paid £100,000 a year.

Railways were being built.

"What is Cobb & Co. going to do now?" people asked.

Cobb & Co. went west, farther and farther west,

away from railway competition. Then came the automobiles.

"That's the end of Cobb & Co.," people said.

But the firm held on, held on right into the motor age of the 1920's. The last coach didn't stop running till 1924.

"It's a sad thing to see Cobb & Co. go," people sighed, remembering.

Something colorful and daring and gay had gone out of the life of Australia.

16 *Ned Kelly and His Outlaw Gang*

Bushranging had nearly passed away. But when gold was discovered, the bushrangers returned. There was much tempting game around. The roads were full of traffic and the travelers were well worth the robbing. It was much easier to hold up a coach or take gold from a digger than to earn money by the sweat of your brow.

In Victoria the bushrangers were mostly ex-convicts from Van Diemen's Land. They were pitiless men whom cruel punishment had warped and twisted. Law was their enemy, not their friend. They got bolder and bolder. One gang held up passers-by not three miles from the center of Melbourne. Another gang boarded a ship as it lay in the harbor, rounded up the crew, and took away a load of gold worth £24,000.

The authorities in Victoria could not put up with that. Experienced officers were brought in from Van Diemen's Land, and they got bushranging under control.

In New South Wales, the gold-age bushranger was a new kind of bandit. He was no transported criminal thirsting for revenge. The "kings of the road" were native-born Australians. They were mostly idle fellows who stole gold and horses from large landowners. They were hard to track down because the back country was home to them. And besides, having grown up in families of poor settlers, they had half the community behind them.

For Australia was still a raw country, and in a raw country people don't have much respect for law. To the poor but proud settlers who were scraping a bare living from the land, the bushrangers seemed heroes fighting the hated police and robbing the rich. The settlers were themselves often just a jump ahead of the law. Men called "bush telegraphs" warned the bandits when police were about.

The roads became utterly unsafe. There was no bold thing the bushranger gangs didn't try. One gang even held up the Eugowra Gold Escort, a coach guarded by four police, and took away £28,-000 in coin and gold.

Something drastic had to be done. In 1867 the government of New South Wales passed a stern law. It said that bushrangers could be killed on sight, along with anybody who hid or helped them in any way. That broke up the gangs and restored order to the roads.

Then in the 1870's, much to the annoyance of the authorities in Victoria, the same kind of bushranger appeared on their side of the hills. It had been the government's boast that such bushrangers as had plagued New South Wales wouldn't last a week in Victoria. But before the colony was done with the Kelly gang, it had cost Victoria £50,000 and several lives. These men were bloody and ruthless. Yet they were such daredevils that their exploits passed into legend and became ballad and story.

Bushrangers terrorized New South Wales and Victoria.

The father of the Kellys was an ex-convict from Van Diemen's Land. He settled in the wild country on the border between New South Wales and Victoria, and there the three Kelly boys rustled cattle and stole horses. Ned, the eldest, alone stole 280 horses.

One day a constable went to the Kelly shack to arrest young Dan for stealing cattle. The family beat up the officer, who later claimed that Ned had shot him in the wrist. Ned and Dan took to the bush with their two pals, Joe Byrne and Steve Hart.

For five months the police hunted the outlaws, but in vain. The gang knew every gully and cave in the hills. Besides, the four Kelly sisters—wild as their brothers—and other relatives and friends in the back country warned them when police were near. At last four mounted troopers did find the gang's camp on Stringybark Creek. But the officers walked into a trap. Three of them were shot down, and only by good luck did the fourth get away.

The murders aroused all Victoria. Big rewards were offered for the killers. A hundred police searched for the young criminals, whose leader, Ned, was only twenty-four. Byrne was twenty-one, Hart eighteen, and Dan Kelly barely seventeen.

After two months the outlaws came out of hiding and carried out a sensational robbery. First they captured a homestead three miles from the town of Euroa and rounded everybody up. Then, while Byrne guarded the thirty prisoners, the other three bushrangers put on stolen clothes, drove to town in a stolen cart, and held up the bank. Along with the loot they took the bank manager and his family. They had to capture two other carts to transport all the prisoners, for besides the manager and his wife and mother-in-law, there were seven children, two servants, and two bank clerks. Going through the town and on to the homestead, the wagons passed many people. But not one of the prisoners dared to call out—such was their fear of the bandits.

At the homestead, the Kelly gang ate a fine dinner. Then they rode away on stolen horses with more than £2000 in cash.

Two months later they crossed the border into New South Wales and carried out a robbery yet more brazen. On a Saturday evening after dark they rode up to the police station in the town of Jerilderie and shouted an alarm. When the two constables who lived there hurried out, they were at once captured. After that Steve Hart kept guard over them while the rest of the gang slept in the policemen's beds. Next day Ned Kelly and Joe Byrne dressed up as constables and strolled about the town with the two policemen.

"If anybody asks who we are," the bushrangers warned them, "you say we are new men who have come to protect the citizens from the Kelly gang."

On Monday morning the outlaws cut the telegraph wires, took over the main room of the Jerilderie hotel, and in leisurely fashion robbed the bank next door. They left with over £2000. Except for the crowd they had locked up inside the hotel, nobody knew that for three days the notorious Kelly gang had been in command of the town.

The rewards for the capture of the gang, dead or alive, rose to £2000 per head. It was the highest price ever offered for any outlaw in Australia. Yet for more than a year nothing was heard of the Kelly gang.

146

Then at last the police managed to bribe one of the "bush telegraphs," a man by the name of Aaron Sherritt. For £4000 he was to lead them to the gang's hide-out. Before he had a chance to do it, however, the Kelly gang killed him. The murder roused the police to new measures. It was decided to send up from Melbourne a special train loaded with troopers who would scour the countryside.

Ned Kelly's answer was to set about wrecking the train. While the crowded express—crammed with troopers, reporters, and anyone else who could get on—was speeding up from Melbourne, the gang captured the little railway town of Glenrowan. They herded thirty people into the small hotel. Then Ned forced linemen to tear up some of the railroad tracks where the line curved along a deep ravine. It would be child's play to shoot up the survivors once the cars were smashed and overturned.

To celebrate the victory he fully expected, Ned called for drinks and music. Many in the hotel secretly admired the killers and entered into the "fun." But one man there resolved to prevent the wholesale murder the gang was planning. It was the local schoolmaster. Working to win Ned Kelly's sympathy for his wife and sister, the man finally got permission to escort them home. As soon as he was out of the hotel, the schoolmaster ran to the tracks and, waving his sister's red scarf in front of a candle, flagged the train just in time to avoid a horrible wreck.

Back at the hotel Ned Kelly was making a speech, telling his "guests" what a wonderful fellow he was, when the train whistle interrupted him.

Ned gave a start. "You'd better go home before the shooting begins," he said. But the landlady urged him to finish his story and, vain as he was heartless, Ned went on talking. By the time he was done, the troopers had arrived at the station.

They advanced on the hotel. But they were cautious about shooting for fear of hitting some of the prisoners inside. As it was, an old man and the landlady's son were killed by stray bullets. Joe Byrne met his end the same way.

The Kellys had invented a "secret weapon." Out of stolen plowshares, they had forced a blacksmith to hammer suits of bullet-proof armor for them. Protected in this way, Hart and Dan Kelly held off the besiegers throughout the night. As for Ned, he had slipped out in his armor to follow a plan of his own. He was going to attack the police in the rear. When that failed, he tried to fight his way back into the hotel. But a sergeant seriously wounded him with a charge of shotgun pellets in the legs. Ned Kelly was taken at last.

"Come out of the hotel!" the police shouted to the prisoners.

They bolted out and threw themselves on the ground. Then one of the troopers crawled forward and set the building on fire. Hart and Dan Kelly perished in the flames.

Ned Kelly was tried and hanged for the Stringybark Creek murders. Thus ended in 1880 the last of the bushrangers. There were holdups on the road once in a while after that, but real bushranging in Australia was over—happily over.

17 *Meat for the World*

When the shepherds rushed off to the gold mines along with all the clerks and sailors and school-teachers and immigrants, the big sheep owners were disturbed.

"We'll be ruined!" they said. "The sheep will die without care."

No more convicts were coming to Australia. There had been such an outcry against them that England had been forced to stop shipping felons to New South Wales. What were the big sheep owners going to do without shepherds?

Gradually a great change came over the sheep

runs. Wire fences replaced post-and-rail ones, while shepherds gave way to mounted men called boundary riders. A man on a horse, riding along the fences to see that everything was in order and safe, was all that was needed. It was better for the sheep and worked out better in profits for the owner.

Cattle had become big business in Australia, too. They had spread to drier and drier areas. After a few years it was a common thing to see overlanders driving herds of cattle into the "outback" where sheep would perish. And a colorful sight the riders were, with their red flannel shirts, high boots, and felt sombreros, sporting emu feathers atop, or broad hats of woven cabbage-tree palm. In their belts were stuck knives and pistols, for there was danger that natives would run off the stock or spear the guards. In their hands the riders flourished fifteen-foot whips that kept the herd together.

Not all the overlanders succeeded. There were desert stretches so hot that oxen hauling carts died standing up. Cattle were a risky business in the "outback" even though, unlike sheep, they could be driven long distances to water. Many a man was ruined before cattlemen learned how to get around drought. But they learned. Cattle could follow the thunderstorms and feed on the grass that sprang up in the wake of the storms.

All this was fine. But between the great sheep runs and the great cattle runs Australia was finding herself with a problem on her hands. Too much meat was being produced. Wool, hides, and tallow —all those could be sent overseas. But meat was

A boundary rider could tend vast herds of sheep.

perishable. It had to be disposed of locally. At a price that allowed the sheepmen and cattlemen a profit, Australians would buy only a certain amount of meat. Of course, meat could be canned and exported, and it was. But what England wanted was *fresh* meat. Her own flocks and herds were dwindling. If only some way could be found of preserving meat without cooking it! The government offered ten thousand acres of land to the man who delivered

the first hundred tons of fresh, uncooked meat to England.

A good many people were working on the problem —and not only in Australia. Between 1849 and 1869, two thousand patents were taken out for the preservation of meat. Somebody was bound to find the answer. It was just a question of time.

Thomas Sutcliffe Mort was one of the people who put his mind on the problem. As a young man in his early twenties, he had come to Sydney from England. He had already engaged successfully in many things, things on a big scale. For no proposition ever seemed too big for Mort to undertake. He had, for instance, started wool sales in Sydney.

"Why," thought this daring immigrant, "should wool be shipped to England and sold there—sometimes for a song? The owner should be present at the sale. Then he can stop it if he doesn't like the price offered."

He told the wool men, "I can get you a better price here, where you can have some say about it, than you will get in England." And so it proved. Be-

154

fore long, buyers were coming from all over the world to buy wool in Sydney and Melbourne. The English merchants didn't like it—but the Australian sheepmen did.

Thomas Mort was interested in railroads and mining. Then he took up dairy farming. He imported special cattle and grass seed and made butter and cheese. For the world's food supply occupied a large part of his thinking. He hated waste. And he saw that waste was nature's way. There was too much food in one place and not enough in another, too much food in one year and not enough in another. "Man ought to be able to balance things," he thought. But—short of cooking and canning perishable food —how could the surplus be preserved and sent where it was needed?

One day he was talking with a friend named Augustus Morris. They were discussing the meat problem. "It seems to me," Morris said, "that the thing to do is to *freeze* the meat. Cold arrests all change. Of course, it's hard to do here, where we have to import ice from America. But there's that French

155

engineer Nicolle. He is making ice by a chemical process. If you want to solve the problem of exporting meat, you ought to get together with him."

So Mort and Nicolle met and started experimenting, Mort supplying the money, Nicolle supplying the skill. They went into the problem deeper and deeper. They started first just chilling the meat. They failed over and over again. A thousand times Mort wished that neither he nor Nicolle nor Morris had ever been born. The experiments had already cost £80,000. Had he a right to risk so large a portion of his children's heritage?

"Yes," he told himself. "For there is no work in the world more important than this in which I am engaged. It means doing away with waste." He went on having faith. Nicolle was working on a plan to use ammonia over and over again in the refrigerator pipes.

In September 1875, Mort believed the problem had been solved. At a luncheon for three hundred guests, he served meat that had been kept frozen for fifteen months. The occasion, he felt, was the high point of his career. He made a speech. He told his guests about the setbacks he and Nicolle had had.

"I knew from the first hour of our experiments," he said, "that truth was at the bottom of the well, but I had no idea the well was so deep." Now the problem of waste had been solved, Mort said. The time had arrived—or it was not far distant—when the various parts of the earth would give forth their products for the use of all.

"God provides enough and to spare for every creature He sends into the world," Mort said, "but conditions are often not in accord. Where food is, the people are not, and where the people are, the food is not. It is within the power of man to adjust these things."

His happy excitement spilled over to all. What a future was opening up for Australia! She was destined to become the great feeder of Europe.

Wealthy sheepmen and cattlemen put up £20,000 for a trial shipment to England. A sailing ship was chartered and fitted with the same kind of ammonia pipes that Mort was using on land. Mort was already tasting the delight of triumph when an unexpected blow struck. The pipes, strained by the movement

157

of the ship, began to leak. The ship could not wait for the repairs to be made, and the meat could not be sent. The experiment had ended before it had begun. Thomas Mort was heartbroken. All his high hopes were dashed. For if the leaks occurred once, why should they not occur every time? The disappointment hastened his end, and he died without seeing the victory.

It came soon afterward. In February 1880 a ship called the *Strathleven* arrived in London with forty tons of beef and mutton. The meat had been frozen on board. It arrived in perfect condition and was sold at high profit. A carcass of lamb was sent to Queen Victoria. A sheep was sent to the Prince of Wales. For this was a historic occasion. From now on England would eat better—and Australia would be the richer for it.

18 *William Farrer*

and the World of Wheat

Thomas Mort had believed that wasteful nature could be controlled. There was someone else in Australia who believed that—a quiet Englishman by the name of William Farrer.

As a young lad Farrer had wanted to become a doctor. To his great disappointment he discovered in his first year at medical school that his health was not strong. So he went out to Australia, where he became a surveyor. But his real interest was his hobby. It was wheat.

Wheat might seem a world away from medicine; yet it was not. Farrer had merely turned his attention from human beings to plants—for in Australia wheat was very sick. It was being swept by a disease called rust. Rust sometimes cut the Australian wheat crop to a tenth of what it should have been. Indeed, in many years Australia did not grow enough wheat to feed the nation, and millers had to import.

Farrer wondered if it was possible to change this. Nature was not an unconquerable power. The answer to rust lay, not in curing the disease, but in helping nature to create new varieties, varieties suited to conditions in Australia.

He set to work breeding wheat. He imported wheat from Canada, from the United States, from Russia. He planted rows of seeds, a hundred in a row, and in the flowering season he crossed the plants. What he wanted above all was to breed a wheat that would ripen early before the hot weather arrived. For it was in the hot weather that rust developed.

It occurred to Farrer that India had a climate much like that of Australia. So he got some Indian varieties of wheat and found that they ripened before the hot weather came on. He crossed them with rust-resistant late varieties. Importing seed from every wheat-growing country in the world, he crossed more and more varieties to get early ripening along with thinness of foliage and richness of gluten. He made hundreds of crosses every year. He was in his fields by 6:30 every morning, and he worked till after dark day after day. And he neatly packaged and labeled with its pedigree every variety he created.

Then came 1889, a terrible year for wheat, the worst that Australian farmers had known. Because of rust alone their losses exceeded £2,000,000. The farmers were in despair, the millers were importing.

The next year Farrer went to a convention held to talk the situation over. He was an unknown man. Nobody had heard of his experiments. When he quietly got up and began to tell about his wheat, everybody was astonished. Many would not believe him when he said he was well on the way to solving

161

the problem of rust. A murmur went through the hall. Some called him a humbug and a charlatan.

Nevertheless the situation was serious. Farrer was later asked to become government wheat experimentalist for New South Wales. He accepted and confidently went on breeding wheat. The hard part of his job was to get balky farmers to co-operate with him, in whom they had no faith. But he had faith. "I am on the high road to doing something of great

Australia learned to grow wheat for the world.

value for one of the most important industries of the country," he told himself. "Sooner or later the world of wheat will follow me."

In his mind's eye he saw Australian fields waving with rich, healthy grain. "This country will be exporting wheat in time," he thought. "For in truth, it is a land wonderfully suited to wheat. Australia has warm soils, wide spaces, temperate climate. All that is necessary is the right variety for each district."

Thousands of discarded packets lay on his shelves. They represented so many disappointments, yet so many steps toward the goal. Farrer was steadily getting there. In the districts where rust had raged, wheat growing had become much less risky. He had early-ripening wheats that tended to escape the rust. He had wheats suited to drier areas, where the disease was seldom a problem. Best of all, he had wheats that would prosper in semi-arid country where people had thought wheat couldn't possibly grow. He was seeing wheat spread into vast southern and western areas, formerly useless, where the rainfall was less than fifteen inches a year.

As the years went on, the fields sown with wheat

multiplied. In 1890 New South Wales had a million acres in wheat; by 1915 she had four million. Undreamed-of things were happening. Australia was even exporting wheat. And her wheat was just as good as that of Canada, the United States, and India.

There were no murmurs now of humbug or charlatan. "Federation," the name that Farrer had given to the improved wheat he had created in 1902, was on every grower's tongue. The farmers knew whom they had to thank. A quiet, persistent man named William Farrer had launched Australia on a new world venture.

19 *One Continent, One Country*

Much of Australia is desert and stone and useless land. It is a hard country. It is a land of vast and difficult spaces. For the most part, its story is the story of the conquest of those spaces.

The mysterious land called, and brave men answered. Some of the explorers struggled back to civilization, others vanished, none knew where. Rescue parties brought home the bodies of still others. But always, in the wake of the explorers, settlers went out and conquered parts of the land. They learned to understand the continent. To a certain extent they learned to control nature. Irrigation turned some of the waste regions into gardens of paradise. Artesian wells made other desert land suitable for flocks and herds.

But more than a hundred years after Cook's discovery of Botany Bay, Australia was still a difficult land, still a land of vast spaces. Half a dozen great cities had sprung up along the coast, but most of the country was almost empty. Half the country's population was in those six cities. People on the east coast in Brisbane felt terribly far from people on the west coast in Perth. In between there were few railroads. And many of the roads were just bush tracks, just wheel-marked lines that washed out in the floods. Motor cars had not yet come. Airplanes were undreamed of. Men still used bullocks, horses, mules, donkeys.

And yet the people on one coast felt very close to those on the other. For *only* space separated them. All spoke the same language. Most had either come from Great Britain or been born in Australia. True, there were six different colonies—New South Wales, Victoria, Tasmania, Queensland, South Australia, and Western Australia. But, except for the mountain

167

range between New South Wales and Victoria and the strait cutting off Tasmania, the boundaries were mostly imaginary lines.

"Of course, we are loyal to our own colony," people said, "but we feel ourselves first of all to be Australians."

Thousands of miles from Mother England, they had a feeling of being apart and yet together, a feeling of "mateship," which the gold diggings had done much to create. Pulling sometimes together, sometimes apart, they had nevertheless succeeded under very hard conditions in transforming a miserable convict colony into a thriving nation. They had a sense of adventure in which all had shared, a sense of common history, of common destiny.

"Why don't we unite and make the continent really one nation?" some asked.

There was much talk of federation, but for a long time it came to nothing. Each colony went its own way. The long-established colony of New South Wales didn't see any advantage for herself in union. If she couldn't boss everything, she didn't want to join.

Tasmania and South Australia were reluctant. If the less-populated colonies didn't have equal rights with the others, they would stay out.

Western Australia wanted some special money arrangements. And a railway must be built to connect her with the eastern states.

But little by little the differences were ironed out, for the people were by this time clamoring for union. "We don't want to be colonists any more!" they insisted. "We want to be Australians!"

And so on January 1, 1901, Queen Victoria signed the document which gave the island continent a federal government—the Commonwealth of Australia. The people had had their will. The whole land was a single nation.

As yet there was no capital city. It was decided, therefore, that the great Exhibition Building in Melbourne should house the Federal Parliament. And that same year old Queen Victoria's grandson, who would one day be King George V of England, himself opened the First Parliament. Twelve thousand important people from all over the country were present. Afterward the entire population of Melbourne shouted itself hoarse at the celebrations, and not one there but felt he had witnessed the greatest event of his time.

The twentieth century had just begun. Australia was entering the new era as a great nation.

Hell.

Some Important Dates of Australian History

1605-06 First Dutch sightings of the coast
1616   Arrival of Dutch ship *Eendracht* at western coast
1642   Abel Tasman's discovery of Van Diemen's Land (Tasmania)
1688   William Dampier's landing on northwest coast
1770   Captain Cook's discovery of New South Wales
1788   Foundation of first settlement (Sydney) by Governor Arthur Phillip
1789   Establishment of New South Wales Corps
1792   End of Phillip's governorship
1802   First Australian wool taken to England by John Macarthur
1803   Circumnavigation of Australia by Sir Matthew Flinders

1807   Arrest of John Macarthur

1808   Rum Corps Rebellion; imprisonment of Governor Bligh

1813   First exploration west of the Blue Mountains

1817-18 Oxley's exploration of the Macquarie and Lachlan rivers

1825   Van Diemen's Land (Tasmania) became a separate colony

1826   Capture of Matthew Brady and his gang

1827   All of Australia claimed as British territory

1828-30 Captain Sturt's exploration of the Darling and Murray rivers

1830   Governor Arthur's "Black Drive" against the Tasmanians

1835   John Batman's treaty with the natives of Port Phillip; foundation of Melbourne

1836   Port Phillip district declared open for settlement

1844-45 Captain Sturt's journey to the interior

1851   Victoria became a separate colony

1851   Discovery of gold in Victoria

1854   Battle at the Eureka Stockade

1859   Queensland became a separate colony

1860   John McDouall Stuart's exploration to the center of the continent

1862   Stuart's crossing of the continent from south to north

1869   Finding of the "Welcome Stranger" gold nugget in Victoria

1872   Completion of telegraph across the continent from south to north

1880   Capture of the Kelly gang

1880   Delivery of first frozen meat to England

1883   Completion of railway between Victoria and New South Wales

1889   Completion of railway between Sydney and Brisbane

1898   William Farrer's appointment as government wheat experimentalist, New South Wales

1901   Establishment of the federal Commonwealth of Australia

Index

Index

Index

LANDMARK BOOKS

WORLD LANDMARK BOOKS